NATIONAL GEOGRAPHIC KiDS

BEGINNER'S WORLD ATLAS

NATIONAL GEOGRAPHIC
WASHINGTON, D.C.

Contents

Understanding Your World

This atlas uses maps and photographs to reveal the wonderful diversity of people, cultures, and the natural world that makes each place on Earth unique. Look for examples of diversity in the land and the people, ranging from traditional to modern lifestyles and from animals in the wild to bustling cities.

Making the Round Earth Flat

From your backyard Earth probably looks flat. If you could travel into space like an astronaut, you would see that Earth is a giant ball with blue oceans, greenish brown land, and white clouds. Even in space you can see only the part of Earth facing you. To see the whole Earth at one time, you need a map. Maps take the round Earth and make it flat, so you can see all of it at one time.

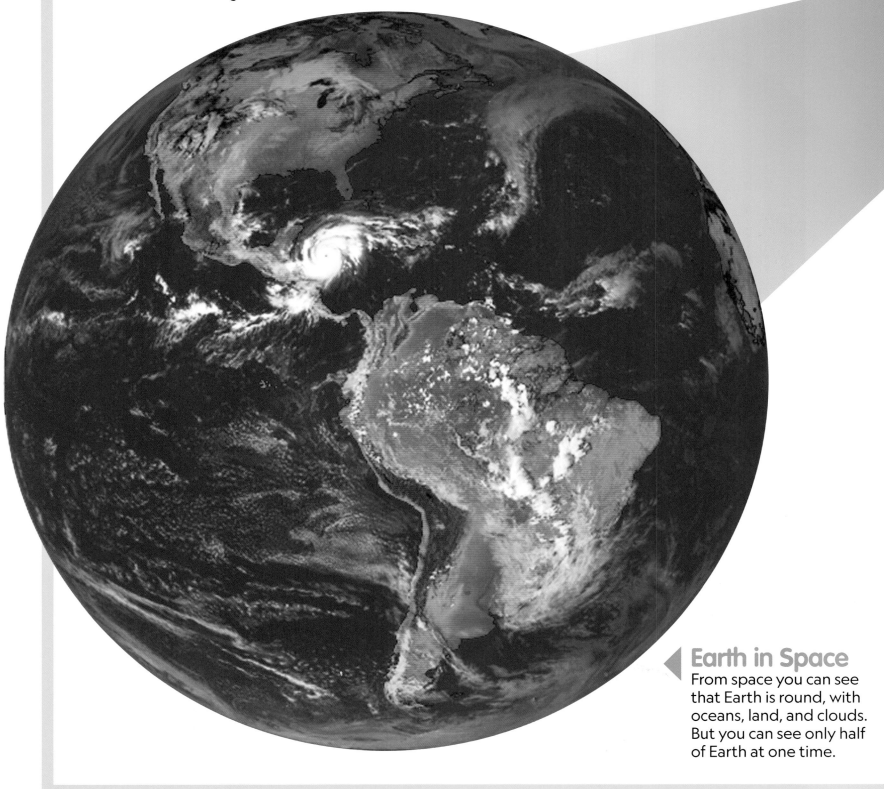

Earth in Space
From space you can see that Earth is round, with oceans, land, and clouds. But you can see only half of Earth at one time.

Earth as a Globe

A globe is a tiny model of Earth that you can put on a stand or hold in your hand. You still can't see all of Earth at one time. You have to turn the globe to see the other side.

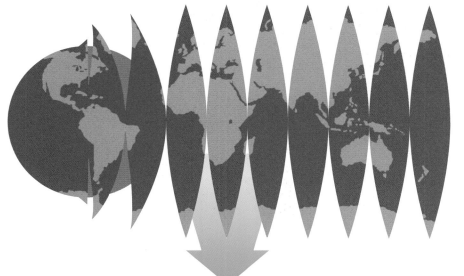

Earth on Paper

If you could peel a globe like an orange, you could make Earth flat, but there would be spaces between the pieces. Mapmakers stretch the land and the water at the top and bottom to fill in the spaces. This is how a map lets you see the whole world all at once.

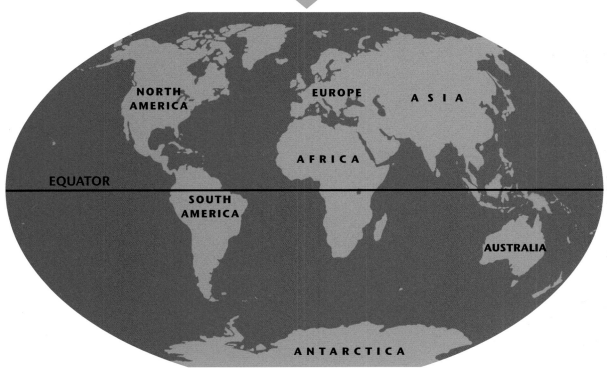

NORTH AMERICA

EUROPE

ASIA

AFRICA

EQUATOR

SOUTH AMERICA

AUSTRALIA

ANTARCTICA

The Equator

The Equator is an imaginary line around Earth's middle. It divides the world into two halves—the Northern Hemisphere and the Southern Hemisphere.

What Is a Map?

A map is a drawing of a place as it looks from above. It is flat, and it is smaller than the place it shows. A map can help you find where you are and where you want to go.

Mapping your backyard ...

... from the ground
From your backyard you see everything in front of you straight on. You have to look up to see your roof and the tops of trees. You can't see what's in front of your house.

... from higher up
From higher up you look down on things. You can see the tops of trees and things in your yard and into the yards of other houses in your neighborhood.

Finding Places on the Map

A map can help you get where you want to go. A map tells you how to read it by showing you a compass rose, a scale, and a key.

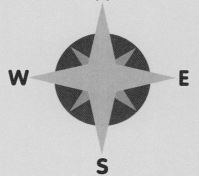

 A compass rose helps you travel in the right direction. It tells you where north (N), south (S), east (E), and west (W) are on your map.

 Some maps have only a north arrow.

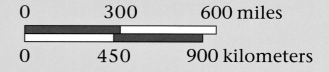

 In the scale above, the upper bar represents distance in miles. The lower bar represents distance in kilometers.

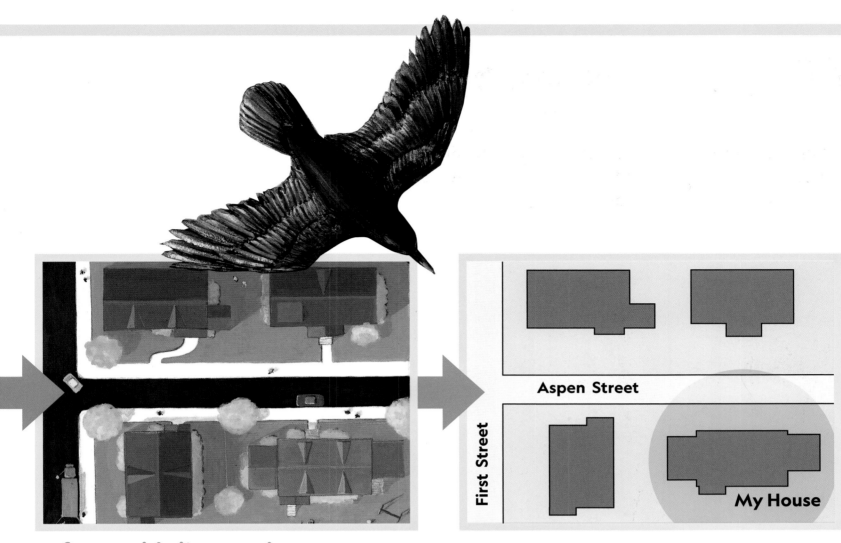

... from a bird's-eye view

If you were a bird flying directly overhead, you would see only the tops of things. You wouldn't see walls, tree trunks, tires, or feet.

... on a map

A map looks at places from a bird's-eye view. But it uses drawings called symbols to show things that don't move, such as these houses.

A map key helps you understand symbols used on the map to show things like mountains, deserts, grasslands, or boundaries.

Map Key

- Mountain
- Desert
- Coniferous forest
- Deciduous forest
- Rain forest
- Grassland
- Wetland
- Tundra
- Volcano
- Dry salt lake
- — Europe-Asia boundary

What This Atlas Will Teach You

You hold the world in your hands as you turn the pages of this atlas. Physical maps will show you natural features, and political maps will show you countries and other places created by people.

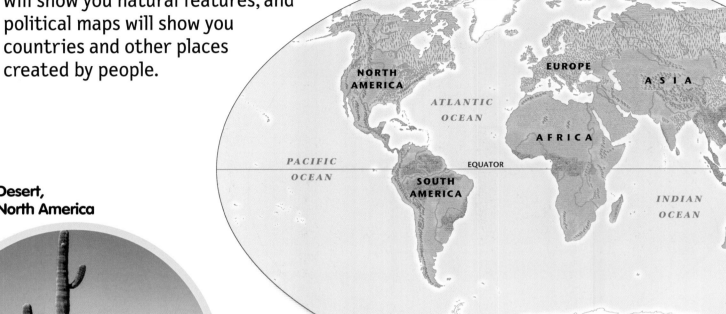

Desert, North America

Coral reef, Pacific Ocean

THE PHYSICAL WORLD

 Land regions You will find out what kinds of land cover a continent. Does it have mountains and deserts? If so, where are they?

 Water You will learn about a continent's chief lakes, rivers, and waterfalls. You'll see that some continents have more water than others.

 Climate Climate is the weather of a place over many years. Some continents are colder and wetter or hotter and drier than others.

 Plants You'll discover what kinds of plants grow on a particular continent.

 Animals Continents each have certain kinds of animals. Did you know that tigers live in the wild only in Asia?

Mountains,
Asia

Sugarcane farmer,
Malawi

Eurostar train,
Europe

ARCTIC OCEAN

Greenland
(Denmark)

NORWAY
ICELAND
FINLAND   R U S S I A

CANADA   UNITED
KINGDOM

FRANCE   UKRAINE KAZAKHSTAN MONGOLIA

UNITED   SPAIN
STATES   TURKEY   JAPAN
MOROCCO   SYRIA   IRAN   C H I N A   PACIFIC

MEXICO   ALGERIA LIBYA EGYPT   OCEAN
                    SAUDI   INDIA
CUBA   ARABIA   VIETNAM

NICARAGUA   VENEZUELA   CHAD SUDAN   THAILAND   PHILIPPINES
            GUYANA MAURITANIA MALI NIGER
COLOMBIA   SURINAME   LIBERIA   ETHIOPIA
PACIFIC   ECUADOR   NIGERIA DEMOCRATIC SOMALIA
                              REPUBLIC   EQUATOR
OCEAN   PERU   BRAZIL   OF THE TANZANIA   INDONESIA   PAPUA
                              CONGO   NEW GUINEA
        BOLIVIA   ANGOLA ZAMBIA
        PARAGUAY   NAMIBIA   MADAGASCAR
                         SOUTH   AUSTRALIA
CHILE   URUGUAY   AFRICA   INDIAN
        ARGENTINA   OCEAN
                                        NEW
                                        ZEALAND

ATLANTIC OCEAN

A N T A R C T I C A

Vancouver,
Canada

THE POLITICAL WORLD

Countries You will learn about the countries that make up a continent. Maps in this atlas show country names in type like this: **UNITED STATES.**

Cities You will find out which cities are the most populous on a continent. The map key will tell you which cities are capitals.

People You will learn where groups of people on a continent come from, where they live, what they do, how they have fun, and more.

Languages Many languages are spoken on most continents. Here you will find out which languages most people speak.

Schoolgirls,
Vietnam

The Physical World

A physical map uses symbols to show where mountains, deserts, forests, and other features of the land are.

The map key tells what the symbols on the map mean.

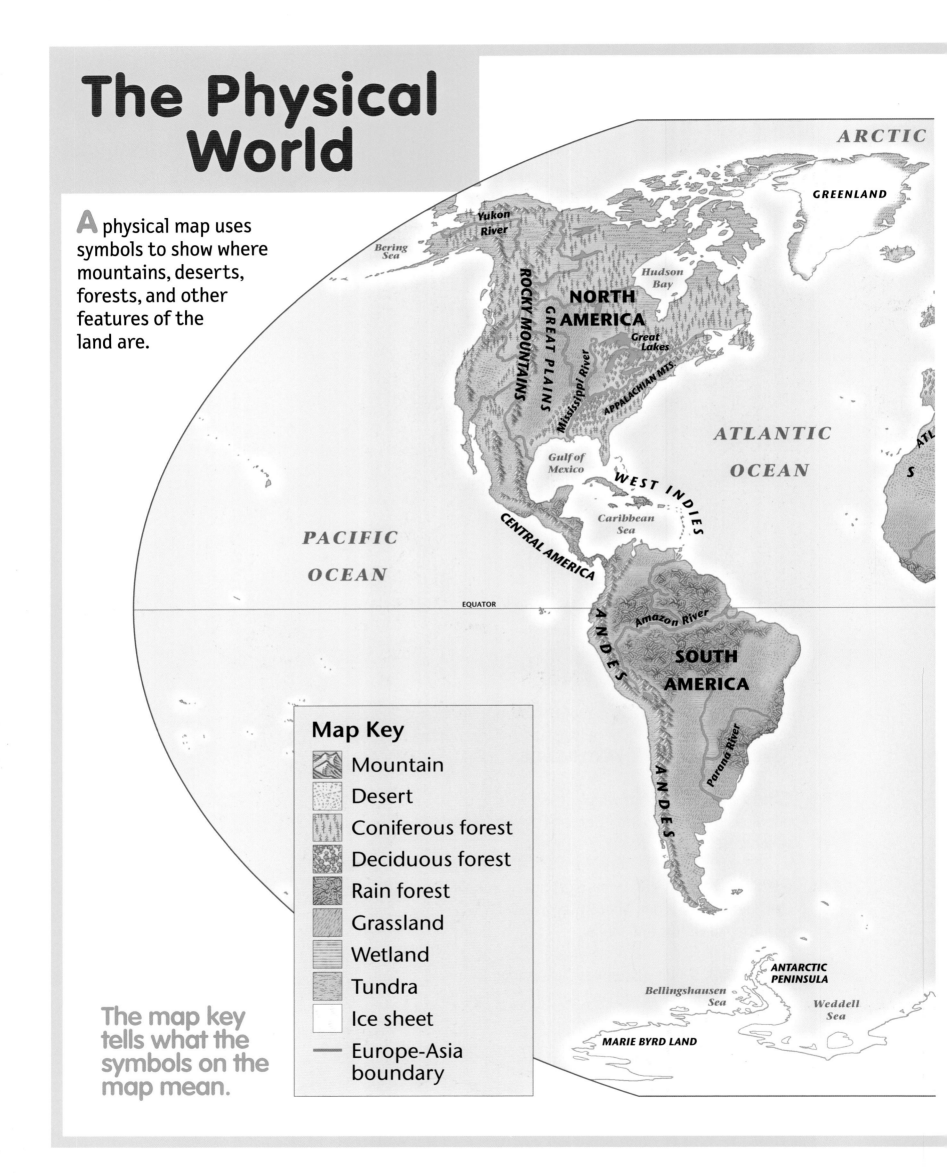

ARCTIC

GREENLAND

Bering Sea

Yukon River

Hudson Bay

ROCKY MOUNTAINS

GREAT PLAINS

NORTH AMERICA

Great Lakes

Mississippi River

APPALACHIAN MTS.

ATLANTIC OCEAN

ATL

S

Gulf of Mexico

WEST INDIES

Caribbean Sea

CENTRAL AMERICA

PACIFIC OCEAN

EQUATOR

ANDES

Amazon River

SOUTH AMERICA

Paraná River

ANDES

ANTARCTIC PENINSULA

Bellingshausen Sea

Weddell Sea

MARIE BYRD LAND

Map Key

- Mountain
- Desert
- Coniferous forest
- Deciduous forest
- Rain forest
- Grassland
- Wetland
- Tundra
- Ice sheet
- — Europe-Asia boundary

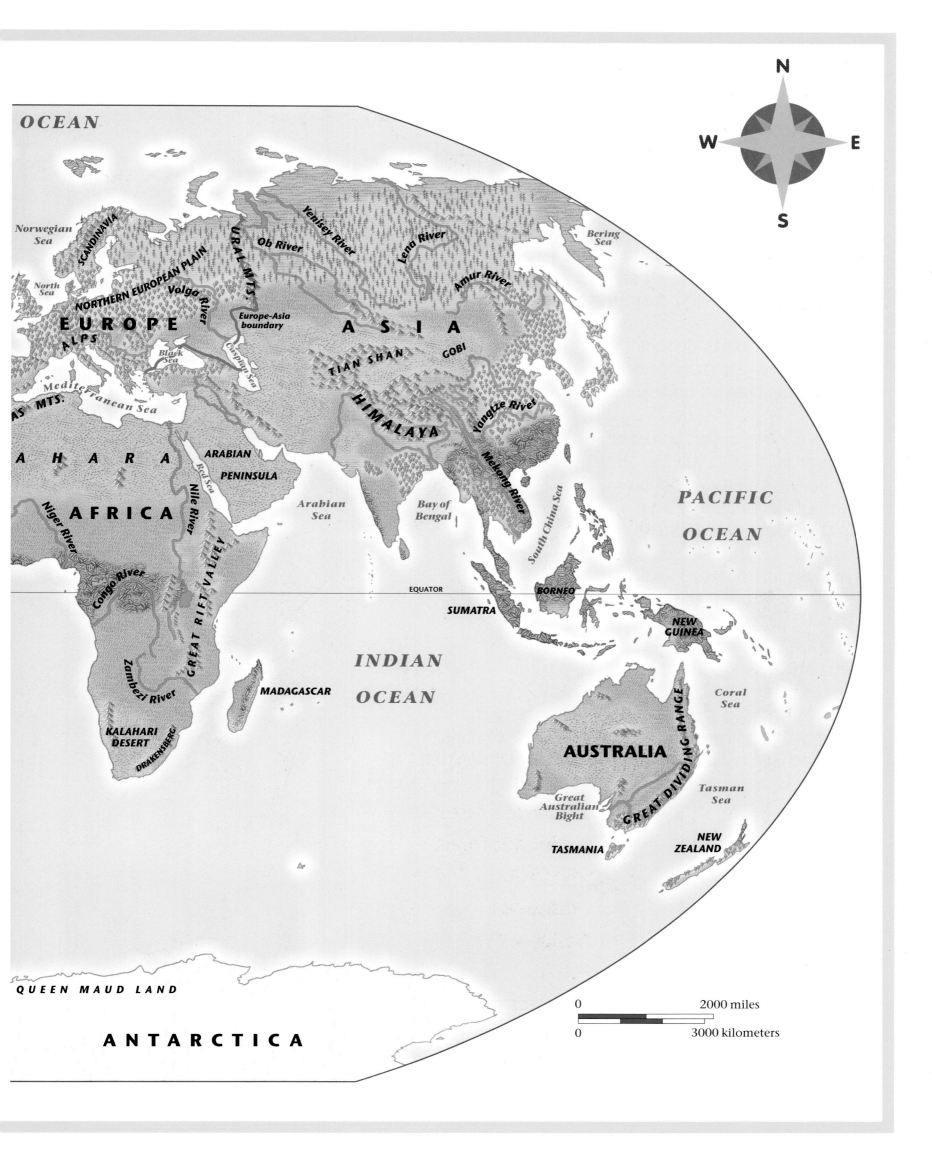

OCEAN

N
W • E
S

Norwegian Sea

SCANDINAVIA

Yenisey River

Ob River

Lena River

Bering Sea

North Sea

NORTHERN EUROPEAN PLAIN

URAL MTS.

Volga River

Amur River

EUROPE

Europe-Asia boundary

A S I A

ALPS

Black Sea

Caspian Sea

TIAN SHAN

GOBI

Mediterranean Sea

S MTS.

HIMALAYA

Yangtze River

A H A R A

ARABIAN

PACIFIC

Red Sea

PENINSULA

Mekong River

Nile River

Arabian Sea

Bay of Bengal

OCEAN

AFRICA

Niger River

GREAT RIFT VALLEY

South China Sea

Congo River

EQUATOR

BORNEO

SUMATRA

NEW GUINEA

Zambezi River

MADAGASCAR

INDIAN

NEW ZEALAND

KALAHARI DESERT

OCEAN

Coral Sea

DRAKENSBERG

GREAT DIVIDING RANGE

AUSTRALIA

Tasman Sea

Great Australian Bight

QUEEN MAUD LAND

TASMANIA

NEW ZEALAND

0   2000 miles

0   3000 kilometers

ANTARCTICA

The Physical World Close Up

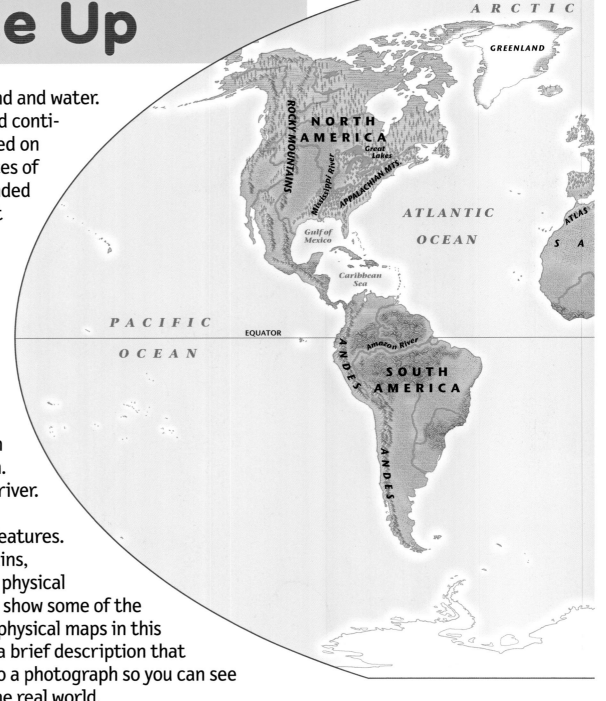

Earth's surface is made up of land and water. The biggest landmasses are called continents. All seven of them are named on this map. Islands are smaller pieces of land that are completely surrounded by water. Greenland is the largest island. A peninsula is land that is almost entirely surrounded by water. Europe has lots of them.

Oceans are the largest bodies of water on Earth. Can you find all four oceans? Lakes are bodies of water surrounded by land, like the Great Lakes, in North America. A river is a large stream that flows into a lake or an ocean. The Nile, in Africa, is the longest river.

These are Earth's main physical features. But continents also have mountains, deserts, forests, and many other physical features. The map symbols below show some of the features that will appear on the physical maps in this atlas. Each symbol is followed by a brief description that explains its meaning. There is also a photograph so you can see what each feature looks like in the real world.

 Mountain
Land rising at least 1,000 feet (305 m) above Earth's surface

 Desert
Very dry land that can be hot or cold and sandy or rocky

 Coniferous forest
Forest with trees that have seed cones and often needlelike leaves

OCEAN

EUROPE

URAL MTS.

Volga River

Europe-Asia boundary

ASIA

ALPS

Mediterranean Sea

MTS.

Gobi

HIMALAYA

Yangtze River

HARA

AFRICA

Nile River

PACIFIC OCEAN

EQUATOR

INDIAN OCEAN

AUSTRALIA

GREAT DIVIDING RANGE

ANTARCTICA

0   2000 miles

0   3000 kilometers

Ice sheet
A permanent layer of thick ice that covers the land, as in Antarctica

Tundra
A cold region with low plants that grow only during warm months

Wetland
Land, such as a marsh or swamp, that is mostly covered with water

Deciduous forest
Forest with trees that change colors and lose leaves in the fall

Rain forest
Forest that needs lots of water and has trees up to 200 feet (61 m) tall

Grassland
A grass-covered area with too little rain for many trees to grow

The Political World

Political maps show places where people live. This one names countries and territories of the world.

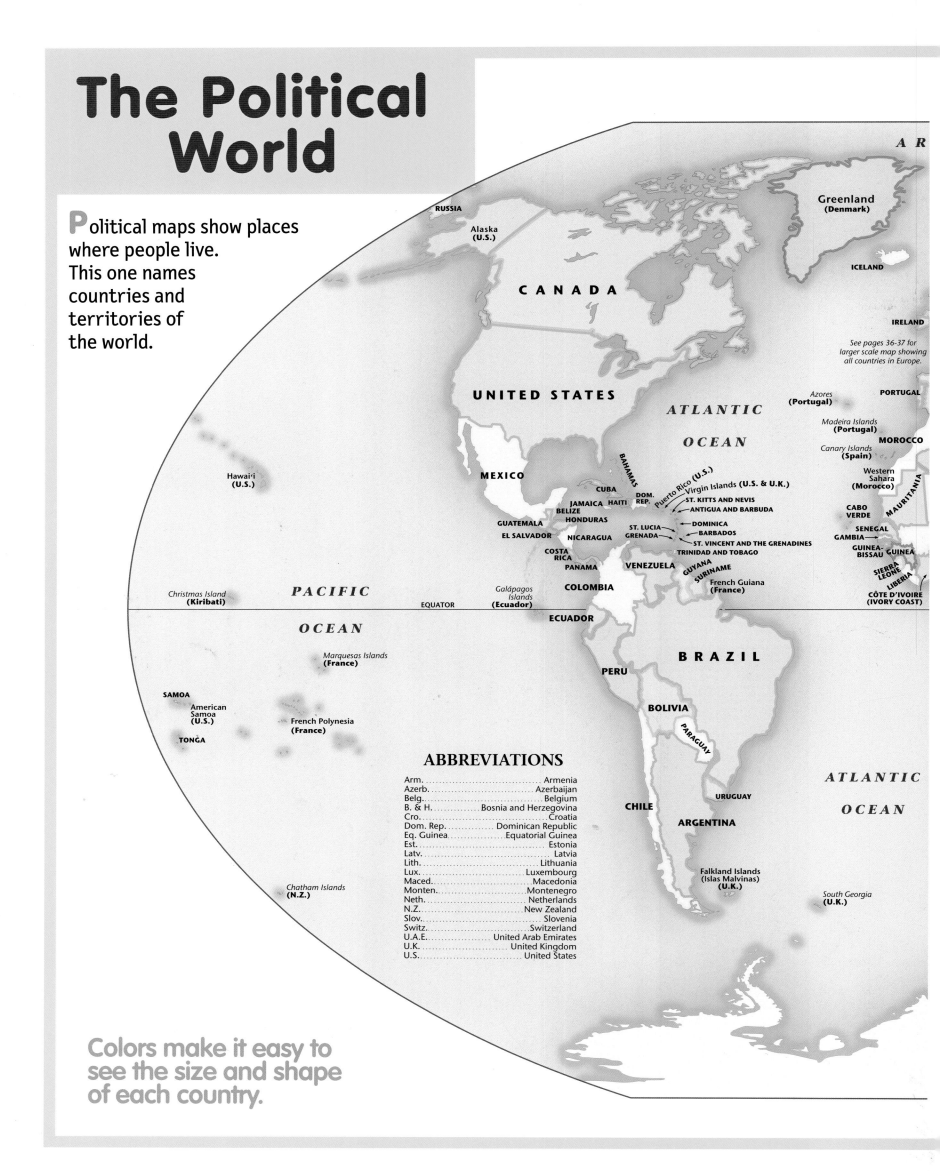

A R

RUSSIA

Greenland
(Denmark)

Alaska
(U.S.)

ICELAND

CANADA

IRELAND

See pages 36-37 for larger scale map showing all countries in Europe.

UNITED STATES

ATLANTIC

Azores
(Portugal)

PORTUGAL

OCEAN

Madeira Islands
(Portugal)

MOROCCO

Hawai'i
(U.S.)

MEXICO

BAHAMAS

Canary Islands
(Spain)

Western
Sahara
(Morocco)

CUBA

Puerto Rico (U.S.)

Virgin Islands (U.S. & U.K.)

MAURITANIA

DOM.
REP.

ST. KITTS AND NEVIS

CABO
VERDE

JAMAICA   HAITI

ANTIGUA AND BARBUDA

BELIZE

DOMINICA

SENEGAL

GUATEMALA

HONDURAS

GAMBIA

EL SALVADOR

NICARAGUA

ST. LUCIA

BARBADOS

GUINEA-

GUINEA

GRENADA

ST. VINCENT AND THE GRENADINES

BISSAU

COSTA
RICA

TRINIDAD AND TOBAGO

SIERRA

PANAMA

VENEZUELA

GUYANA

LEONE

LIBERIA

SURINAME

French Guiana
(France)

CÔTE D'IVOIRE
(IVORY COAST)

COLOMBIA

Christmas Island
(Kiribati)

PACIFIC

Galápagos Islands
(Ecuador)

EQUATOR

ECUADOR

OCEAN

Marquesas Islands
(France)

B R A Z I L

PERU

SAMOA

American
Samoa
(U.S.)

BOLIVIA

French Polynesia
(France)

PARAGUAY

TONGA

ABBREVIATIONS

Arm.	Armenia
Azerb.	Azerbaijan
Belg.	Belgium
B. & H.	Bosnia and Herzegovina
Cro.	Croatia
Dom. Rep.	Dominican Republic
Eq. Guinea	Equatorial Guinea
Est.	Estonia
Latv.	Latvia
Lith.	Lithuania
Lux.	Luxembourg
Maced.	Macedonia
Monten.	Montenegro
Neth.	Netherlands
N.Z.	New Zealand
Slov.	Slovenia
Switz.	Switzerland
U.A.E.	United Arab Emirates
U.K.	United Kingdom
U.S.	United States

ATLANTIC

URUGUAY

OCEAN

CHILE

ARGENTINA

Chatham Islands
(N.Z.)

Falkland Islands
(Islas Malvinas)
(U.K.)

South Georgia
(U.K.)

Colors make it easy to see the size and shape of each country.

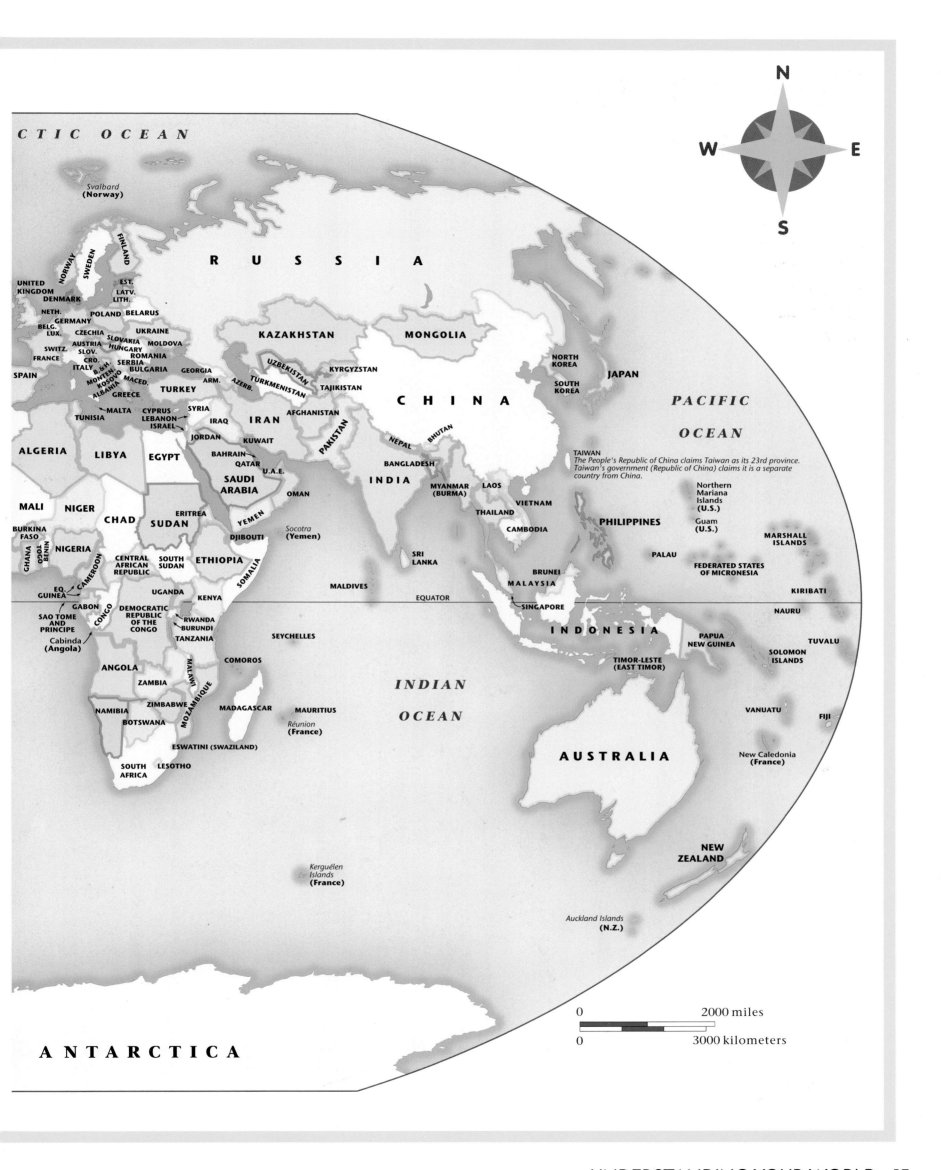

N
W **E**
S

CTIC OCEAN

Svalbard
(Norway)

R U S S I A

NORWAY
SWEDEN
FINLAND
UNITED
KINGDOM
DENMARK
EST.
LATV.
LITH.
NETH.
GERMANY
POLAND BELARUS
BELG.
LUX.
CZECHIA
SWITZ. AUSTRIA HUNGARY
FRANCE SLOV.
CRO.
ITALY SERBIA
B.&H.
MONTEN.
KOSOVO MACED.
ALBANIA GREECE
SLOVAKIA
MOLDOVA
ROMANIA
BULGARIA
GEORGIA
ARM.
AZERB.
SPAIN
TURKEY
MALTA CYPRUS SYRIA
TUNISIA LEBANON
ISRAEL IRAQ
JORDAN
BAHRAIN
QATAR
U.A.E.
OMAN
YEMEN
IRAN
AFGHANISTAN
PAKISTAN

KAZAKHSTAN
UZBEKISTAN
TURKMENISTAN
KYRGYZSTAN
TAJIKISTAN

MONGOLIA

C H I N A

NORTH
KOREA
SOUTH
KOREA
JAPAN

PACIFIC

OCEAN

TAIWAN
*The People's Republic of China claims Taiwan as its 23rd province.
Taiwan's government (Republic of China) claims it is a separate
country from China.*

ALGERIA LIBYA EGYPT
SAUDI
ARABIA

MALI
NIGER
CHAD
SUDAN
ERITREA
DJIBOUTI
BURKINA
FASO
GHANA TOGO
BENIN
NIGERIA
CAMEROON
CENTRAL
AFRICAN
REPUBLIC
SOUTH
SUDAN
ETHIOPIA
SOMALIA
EQ.
GUINEA
GABON CONGO
SAO TOME
AND
PRINCIPE
Cabinda
(Angola)
DEMOCRATIC
REPUBLIC
OF THE
CONGO
UGANDA
RWANDA
BURUNDI
TANZANIA
KENYA

NEPAL BHUTAN
BANGLADESH
INDIA
MYANMAR
(BURMA)
LAOS
THAILAND
VIETNAM
CAMBODIA

PHILIPPINES

Northern
Mariana
Islands
(U.S.)
Guam
(U.S.)

MARSHALL
ISLANDS

PALAU
FEDERATED STATES
OF MICRONESIA

KIRIBATI

Socotra
(Yemen)

SRI
LANKA

MALDIVES
EQUATOR

BRUNEI
MALAYSIA
SINGAPORE

NAURU

ANGOLA
ZAMBIA
MALAWI
MOZAMBIQUE
NAMIBIA ZIMBABWE
BOTSWANA
ESWATINI (SWAZILAND)
SOUTH LESOTHO
AFRICA

SEYCHELLES

COMOROS
MADAGASCAR
MAURITIUS
Réunion
(France)

I N D O N E S I A
TIMOR-LESTE
(EAST TIMOR)

PAPUA
NEW GUINEA

SOLOMON
ISLANDS

TUVALU

INDIAN

OCEAN

A U S T R A L I A

VANUATU
FIJI
New Caledonia
(France)

Kerguélen
Islands
(France)

NEW
ZEALAND

Auckland Islands
(N.Z.)

0   2000 miles

0   3000 kilometers

A N T A R C T I C A

NORTH AMERICA

North America is shaped like a triangle. It is wide in the north. In the south, it becomes a strip of land only 30 miles (48 km) wide at its narrowest point. There, the Panama Canal connects the Atlantic and Pacific Oceans. The warm islands in the Caribbean Sea are part of North America. So is icy Greenland in the far north. The seven countries between Mexico and South America make up a region commonly called Central America. It connects the rest of North America to South America.

A polar bear roams the icy shore of Hudson Bay in Manitoba, Canada, in search of food.

The Golden Gate Bridge stretches high above the entrance to San Francisco Bay in California, U.S.A.

NORTH AMERICA

LAND REGIONS The Rocky Mountains stretch through western North America into Mexico, where the mountains are called the Sierra Madre Oriental. Older, lower mountains called the Appalachians are in the east. Grassy plains lie between these two mountain chains.

WATER Together, the Mississippi and its tributary the Missouri make up the continent's longest river. The Great Lakes are the world's largest group of freshwater lakes.

CLIMATE The far north is icy cold. Temperatures get warmer as you move south. Deserts cover dry areas in the southwest, but much of Central America is wet and hot.

PLANTS Large forests grow where rain or snow is plentiful. Grasslands cover areas with less precipitation.

ANIMALS There is a big variety of animals—everything from bears, moose, and wolves to monkeys and colorful parrots.

A white-tailed deer nuzzles her babies in a meadow near the Great Lakes. Deer live in almost every country on the continent.

North America is famous for its deciduous forests. Leaves turn fiery colors each fall.

Palm trees grow along sandy beaches on islands in the Caribbean Sea. In this part of North America the weather is warm year-round.

Dragonlike iguanas live in the rain forests of Mexico and Central America. This harmless lizard can grow as long as a man's leg.

Deserts are found in the south-western part of North America. The large rock formation on the right is called The Mitten. Can you guess why?

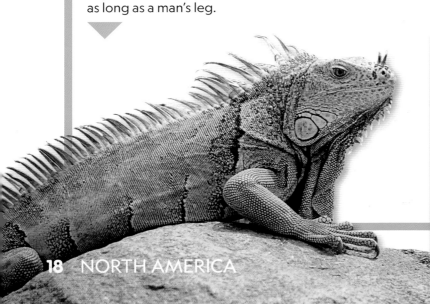

ASIA

Denali
(Mt. McKinley)
Highest point in
North America

N

ARCTIC
OCEAN

G R E E N L A N D

Brooks Range

Yukon
River

Mackenzie River

COAST MOUNTAINS

ROCKY MOUNTAINS

Great
Bear Lake

Great
Slave Lake

Hudson
Bay

This view from a plane shows that Greenland has high mountains and lots of snow and ice.

Cascade Range

Columbia River

Sierra Nevada

G R E A T   P L A I N S

Lake
Winnipeg

Missouri River

Mississippi River

Great Lakes

APPALACHIAN MOUNTAINS

Map Key

Mountain
Desert
Coniferous forest
Deciduous forest
Rain forest
Grassland
Wetland
Tundra
Ice sheet
Volcano
■ Point of interest

Colorado River

Death Valley
Lowest point in
North America

Ohio River

Mississippi River

ATLANTIC
OCEAN

PACIFIC
OCEAN

SIERRA MADRE OCCIDENTAL

SIERRA MADRE ORIENTAL

Rio Grande

Gulf of Mexico

W E S T

I N D I E S

Yucatan
Peninsula

CENTRAL AMERICA

Caribbean Sea

0   600 miles

0   900 kilometers

SOUTH AMERICA

NORTH AMERICA

Snowboarding and skiing are popular sports in mountain areas.

This farmer is harvesting wheat on a big farm in Canada. Canada and the United States grow much of the world's wheat.

COUNTRIES Canada, the United States, Mexico, and the countries of Central America and the West Indies make up North America.

CITIES Mexico City is the most populous city in North America followed by the U.S. cities of New York and Los Angeles. Santo Domingo, in the Dominican Republic, is the most populous city in the West Indies.

PEOPLE Ancestors of most people in North America came from Europe. Many other people trace their roots to Africa and Asia. Various groups of Native Americans live throughout the continent.

LANGUAGES English and Spanish are the main languages. A large number of people in Canada and Haiti speak French. There are also many Native American languages.

The Angel of Independence monument in Mexico City commemorates Mexico's independence from Spain in 1821.

These red berries hold coffee beans. Many farmers in Guatemala make a living growing coffee.

These children from the country of Trinidad and Tobago in the West Indies are dressed up to celebrate a festival called Carnival.

Cliff Palace, part of Mesa Verde National Park, in Colorado, U.S.A., was built long ago by Native Americans. It is the largest cliff dwelling in North America.

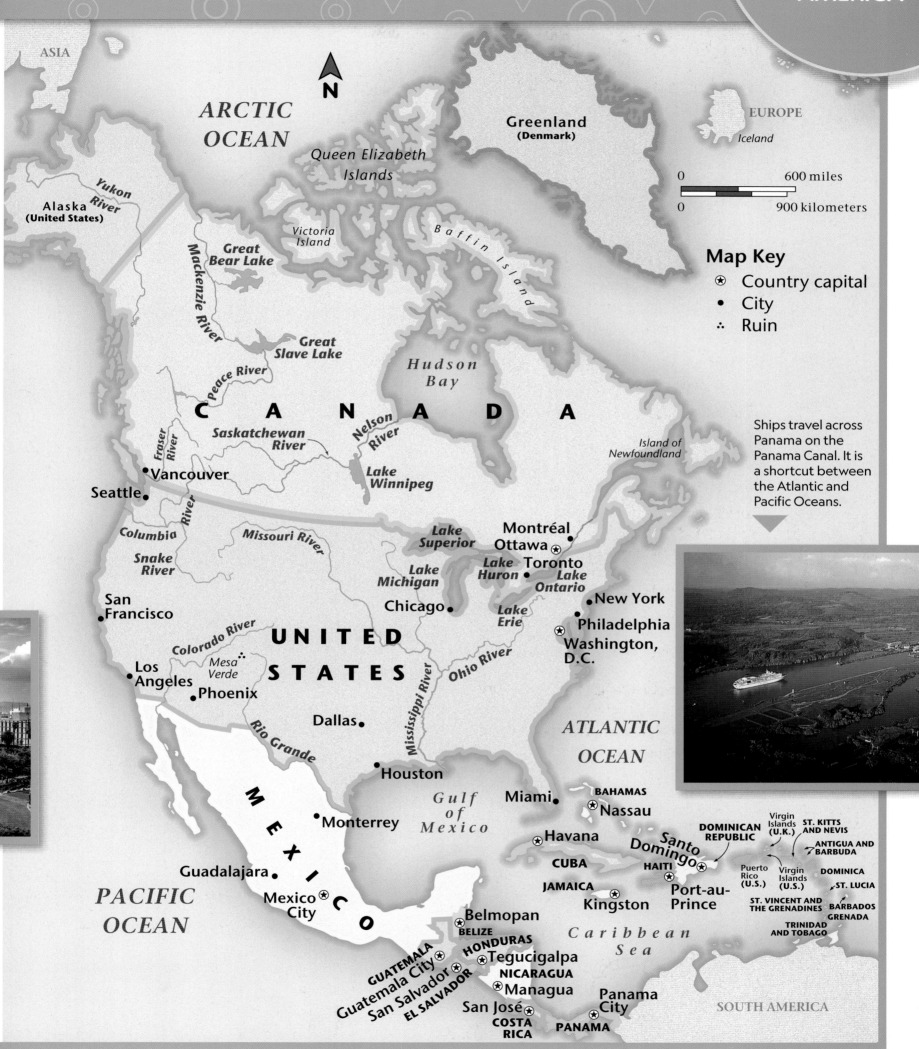

ASIA

ARCTIC OCEAN

Greenland (Denmark)

EUROPE

Iceland

Queen Elizabeth Islands

Yukon River

Alaska (United States)

Victoria Island

Baffin Island

0 — 600 miles
0 — 900 kilometers

Map Key
⊛ Country capital
• City
∴ Ruin

Great Bear Lake

Mackenzie River

Great Slave Lake

Peace River

Hudson Bay

C A N A D A

Fraser River

Saskatchewan River

Nelson River

Island of Newfoundland

Lake Winnipeg

Ships travel across Panama on the Panama Canal. It is a shortcut between the Atlantic and Pacific Oceans.

• Vancouver

Seattle •

Columbia River

Missouri River

Lake Superior

Montréal •
Ottawa ⊛
Lake Huron   Toronto •
Lake Michigan   Lake Ontario

Snake River

San Francisco •

New York •
Lake Erie
Philadelphia ⊛
Washington, D.C.

Chicago •

U N I T E D   S T A T E S

Colorado River

Mesa Verde ∴

Los Angeles •
Phoenix •

Ohio River

ATLANTIC OCEAN

Dallas •

Rio Grande

Mississippi River

Houston •

M E X I C O

Monterrey •

Gulf of Mexico

Miami •

BAHAMAS
Nassau ⊛

Virgin Islands (U.K.)
ST. KITTS AND NEVIS

DOMINICAN REPUBLIC

Havana ⊛

Santo Domingo •

ANTIGUA AND BARBUDA

Guadalajara •

CUBA

HAITI

Puerto Rico (U.S.)

Virgin Islands (U.S.)

DOMINICA

PACIFIC OCEAN

Mexico City ⊛

JAMAICA

Kingston •

Port-au-Prince ⊛

ST. LUCIA

ST. VINCENT AND THE GRENADINES

BARBADOS
GRENADA

Belmopan ⊛
BELIZE

Caribbean Sea

TRINIDAD AND TOBAGO

GUATEMALA
Guatemala City ⊛
San Salvador ⊛
EL SALVADOR

HONDURAS
Tegucigalpa ⊛
NICARAGUA
Managua ⊛

San José ⊛
COSTA RICA

Panama City •

PANAMA

SOUTH AMERICA

UNITED STATES

STATES The United States is made up of 50 states. Alaska and Hawaiʻi are separated from the rest of the country. So you can see them close up, they are shown near the bottom of the map. Use the small globe above to see their real locations.

CITIES Washington, D.C., is the national capital. Each state also has a capital city. New York City has the most people.

PEOPLE People from almost every country in the world live in the United States. Most live and work in and around cities.

LANGUAGES English is the chief language, followed by Spanish.

Sandy beaches, like this one in Delaware, are popular places to visit in the summer.

Chinese New Year is a big celebration in San Francisco, California. Lots of Chinese Americans live there.

Softball is a popular sport in the United States along with baseball, soccer, basketball, and football. This girl is getting ready to swing her bat in a softball game.

A scarecrow stands guard over a field of sunflowers in Kansas.

PACIFIC OCEAN

Seattle
Olympia
WASHINGTON
Portland
Salem
OREGON
Boise
ID

Columbia River

Carson City
Sacramento
San Francisco
NEVADA
San Jose
Las Vegas
Los Angeles
AR
San Diego

ALASKA

Juneau

0   400 miles
0   600 kilometers

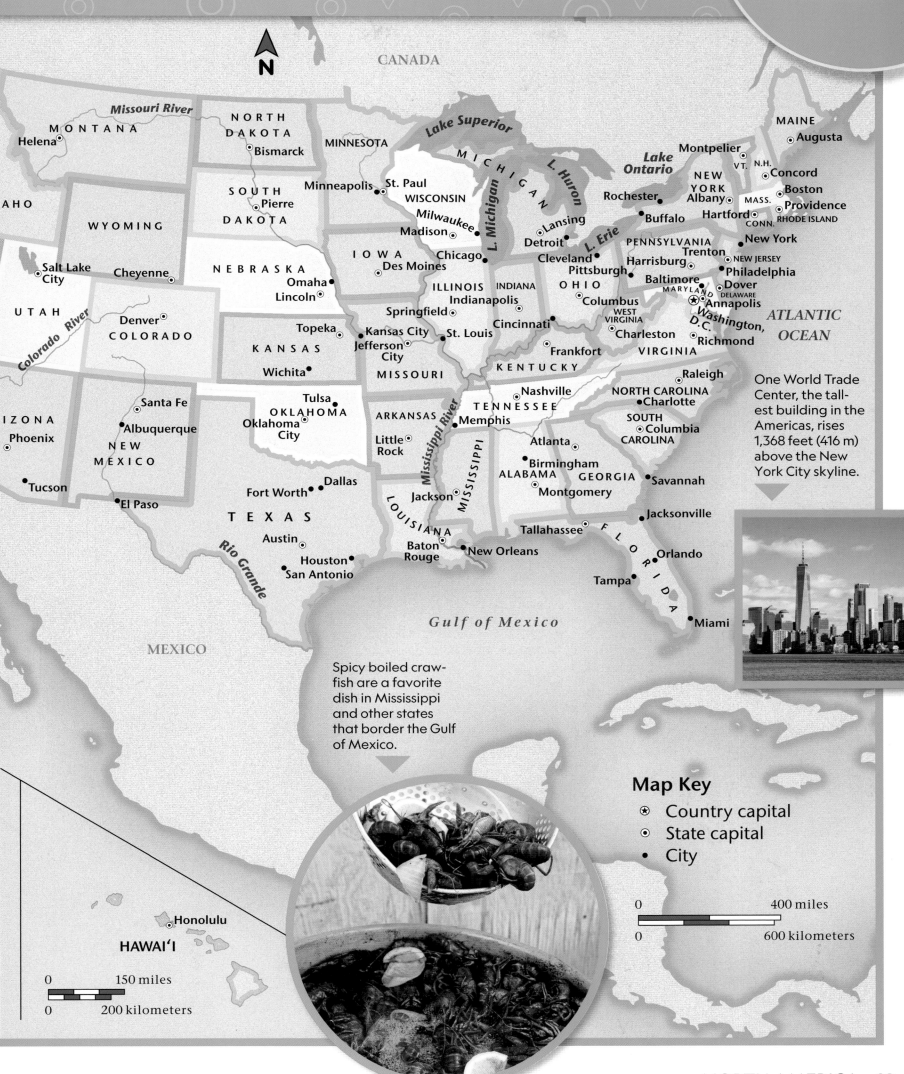

CANADA

N

Missouri River

MONTANA
Helena

NORTH DAKOTA
Bismarck

MINNESOTA
St. Paul
Minneapolis

Lake Superior

MICHIGAN

L. Huron

Lake Ontario

MAINE
Augusta

Montpelier
VT. N.H.
Concord

IDAHO

WYOMING

SOUTH DAKOTA
Pierre

WISCONSIN
Milwaukee
Madison

L. Michigan

Lansing

Rochester

NEW YORK
Albany

MASS.

Boston
Providence

RHODE ISLAND

Salt Lake City

Cheyenne

NEBRASKA
Omaha
Lincoln

IOWA
Des Moines

Chicago

Detroit
Cleveland

L. Erie

Buffalo

Hartford

CONN.

New York

UTAH

Denver
COLORADO

ILLINOIS
Springfield

INDIANA
Indianapolis

OHIO
Columbus

Cincinnati

Pittsburgh

PENNSYLVANIA
Harrisburg

Trenton
NEW JERSEY
Philadelphia

Baltimore
Dover

Colorado River

Topeka
KANSAS
Wichita

Kansas City
Jefferson City

St. Louis

WEST VIRGINIA

MARYLAND
Annapolis
Washington, D.C.

ATLANTIC OCEAN

MISSOURI

Frankfort

Charleston

Richmond

ARIZONA

Santa Fe

Albuquerque

NEW MEXICO

Phoenix

Tucson

El Paso

Tulsa
OKLAHOMA
Oklahoma City

ARKANSAS
Little Rock

KENTUCKY

TENNESSEE
Nashville

Memphis

VIRGINIA

Raleigh
NORTH CAROLINA
Charlotte

SOUTH CAROLINA
Columbia

Mississippi River

Atlanta

Fort Worth
Dallas

TEXAS

Austin

Houston
San Antonio

Rio Grande

Jackson
MISSISSIPPI

LOUISIANA

Baton Rouge
New Orleans

ALABAMA
Montgomery

Birmingham

GEORGIA

Savannah

Tallahassee

FLORIDA

Jacksonville

Orlando

Tampa

Miami

One World Trade Center, the tallest building in the Americas, rises 1,368 feet (416 m) above the New York City skyline.

MEXICO

Gulf of Mexico

Spicy boiled crawfish are a favorite dish in Mississippi and other states that border the Gulf of Mexico.

Map Key
- ✪ Country capital
- ⊙ State capital
- • City

Honolulu

HAWAI'I

0   150 miles
0   200 kilometers

0   400 miles
0   600 kilometers

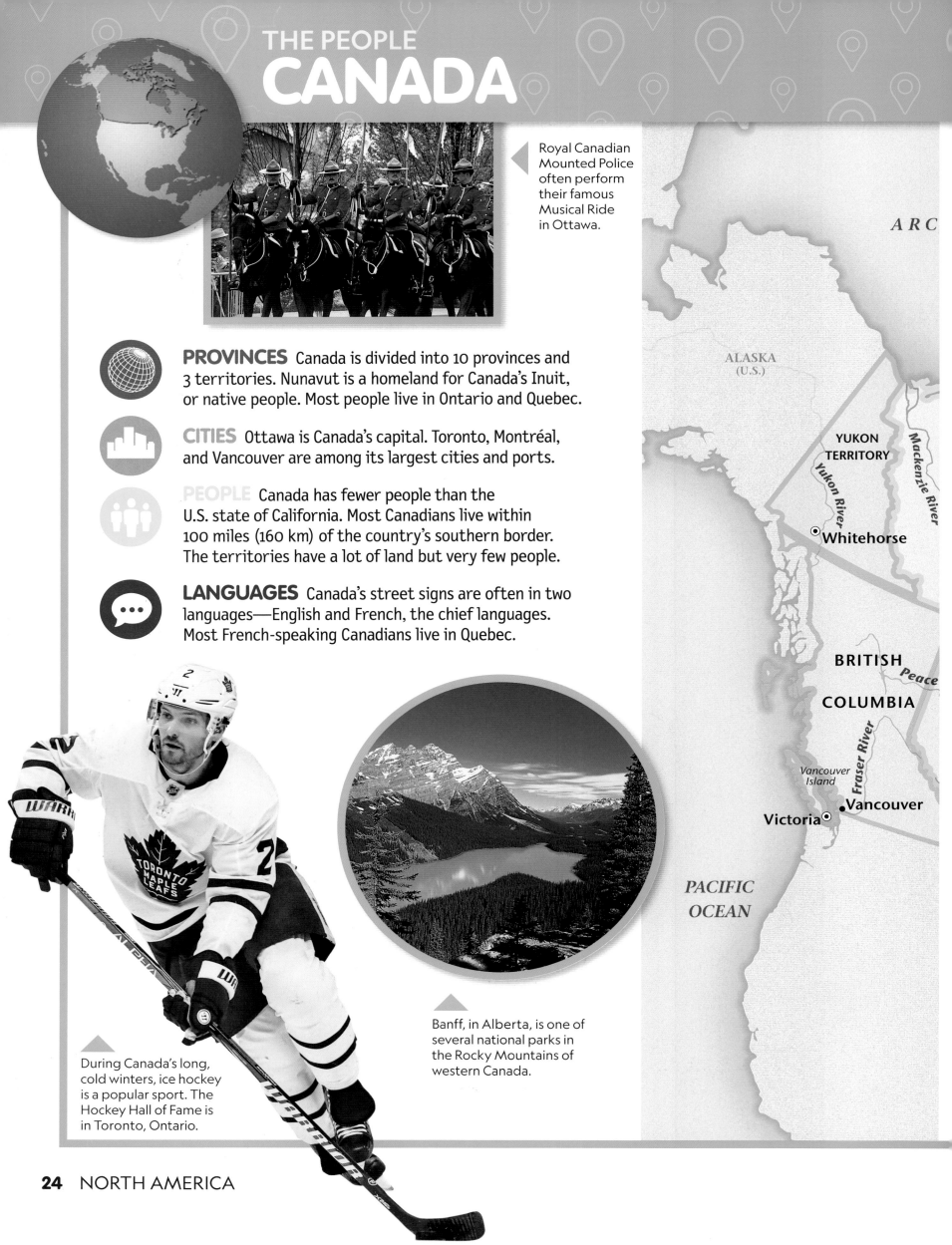

Royal Canadian Mounted Police often perform their famous Musical Ride in Ottawa.

PROVINCES Canada is divided into 10 provinces and 3 territories. Nunavut is a homeland for Canada's Inuit, or native people. Most people live in Ontario and Quebec.

CITIES Ottawa is Canada's capital. Toronto, Montréal, and Vancouver are among its largest cities and ports.

PEOPLE Canada has fewer people than the U.S. state of California. Most Canadians live within 100 miles (160 km) of the country's southern border. The territories have a lot of land but very few people.

LANGUAGES Canada's street signs are often in two languages—English and French, the chief languages. Most French-speaking Canadians live in Quebec.

ALASKA (U.S.)

ARC

YUKON TERRITORY

Mackenzie River

Yukon River

⊙ Whitehorse

BRITISH COLUMBIA

Peace

Fraser River

Vancouver Island

• Vancouver

Victoria ⊙

PACIFIC OCEAN

Banff, in Alberta, is one of several national parks in the Rocky Mountains of western Canada.

During Canada's long, cold winters, ice hockey is a popular sport. The Hockey Hall of Fame is in Toronto, Ontario.

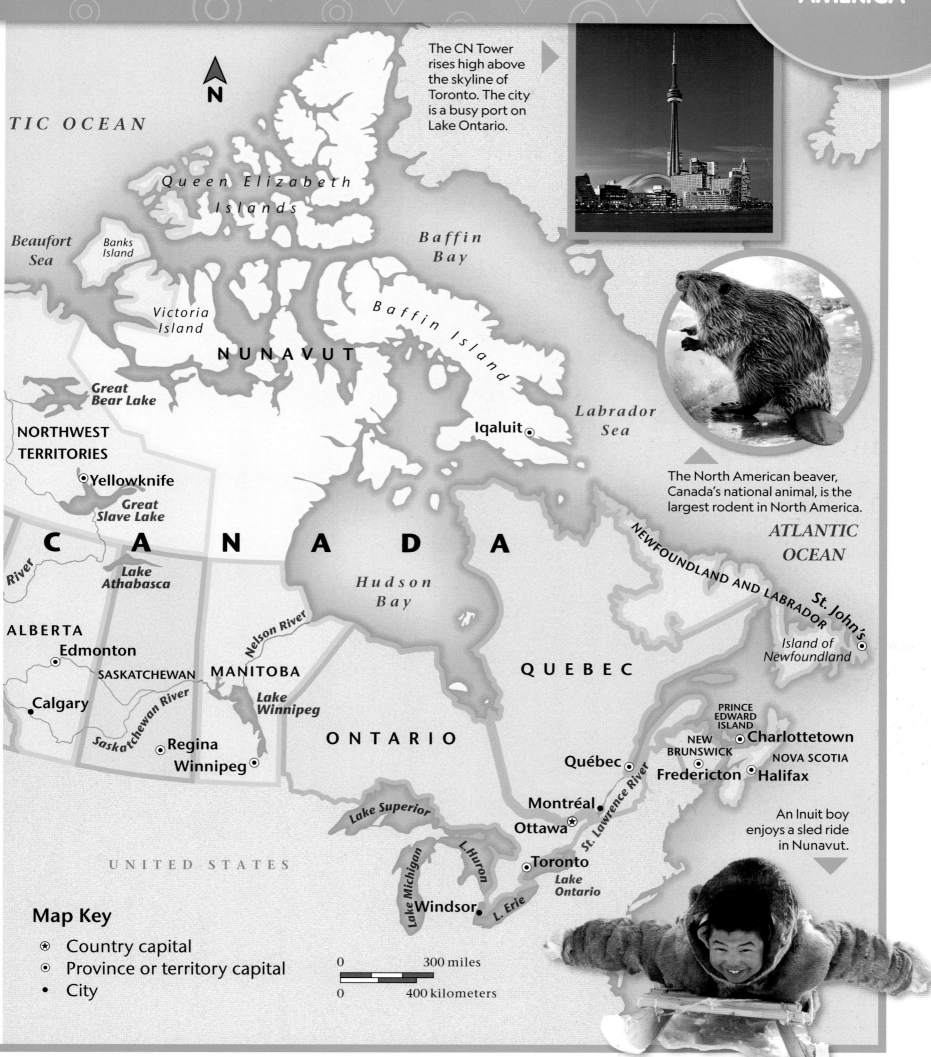

TIC OCEAN

N

The CN Tower rises high above the skyline of Toronto. The city is a busy port on Lake Ontario.

Queen Elizabeth Islands

Beaufort Sea

Banks Island

Baffin Bay

Victoria Island

Baffin Island

NUNAVUT

Great Bear Lake

Labrador Sea

NORTHWEST TERRITORIES

Iqaluit

The North American beaver, Canada's national animal, is the largest rodent in North America.

Yellowknife

Great Slave Lake

C A N A D A

NEWFOUNDLAND AND LABRADOR

ATLANTIC OCEAN

River

Lake Athabasca

Hudson Bay

St. John's

ALBERTA

Island of Newfoundland

Edmonton

Nelson River

SASKATCHEWAN

MANITOBA

QUEBEC

Calgary

Saskatchewan River

Lake Winnipeg

PRINCE EDWARD ISLAND

Regina

ONTARIO

NEW BRUNSWICK

Charlottetown

Winnipeg

Québec

NOVA SCOTIA

Fredericton

Halifax

Lake Superior

Montréal

St. Lawrence River

UNITED STATES

L. Huron

Ottawa

An Inuit boy enjoys a sled ride in Nunavut.

Lake Michigan

Toronto

Lake Ontario

Map Key

⊛ Country capital

◎ Province or territory capital

• City

Windsor

L. Erie

0   300 miles

0   400 kilometers

SOUTH AMERICA

South America is a land of many amazing things, including the world's biggest rain forest (the Amazon) and one of its driest deserts (the Atacama). It has emerald mines, mysterious ruins, and crowded modern cities. In the mountains, camel-like animals called llamas carry heavy loads. On the grasslands, cowboys called gauchos herd cattle. Foods such as potatoes and tomatoes are native to South America.

In the Amazon rain forest, a jaguar sharpens its claws on a tree trunk.

Sugarloaf Mountain rises above Guanabara Bay in Rio de Janeiro, Brazil's second most populous city.

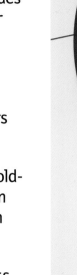

Llamas can carry 50 to 75 pounds (23 to 34 kg) up to 20 miles (32 km) a day in the Andes.

LAND REGIONS Snowcapped mountains called the Andes run along the west coast. Rain forests and grasslands cover much of the rest of the continent. The continent's driest desert lies between the Andes and the Pacific Ocean.

WATER The Amazon River carries more water than any other river in the world. More than 1,000 streams and rivers flow into it. Lake Titicaca is the continent's largest lake.

CLIMATE Much of South America is warm all year. The coldest places are in the Andes and at the continent's southern tip. Each year more than 80 inches (200 cm) of rain falls in the rain forests.

Parts of the Atacama Desert, in northern Chile, have not had rainfall in more than 100 years.

PLANTS The Amazon rain forest has more kinds of plants than any other place in the world. In the south, grasslands feed large herds of cattle and sheep.

ANIMALS Colorful toucans, noisy howler monkeys, and giant snakes live in the rain forests. Sure-footed llamas, huge birds called condors, and guinea pigs live in the Andes. The flightless rhea, which looks like an ostrich, roams the wide southern grasslands.

The world's largest water lilies grow in the Amazon River. They are big enough to hold this young girl.

Imagine living in a place where birds are as big and as colorful as these macaws. They live in the rain forests.

Cold outside and hot inside, snow-covered volcanoes are scattered throughout the Andes.

NORTH AMERICA

Lake Maracaibo

Orinoco River

Angel Falls
Tallest waterfall in the world

N

A M A Z O N

Negro River

Amazon River

Amazon River

EQUATOR

EQUATOR

B A S I N

A
N
D
E
S

PACIFIC

OCEAN

Lake Titicaca

Driest place in the world

Atacama Desert

Paraguay River

Paraná River

Iguazú Falls

ATLANTIC

OCEAN

Mt. Aconcagua
Highest point in South America

A
N
D
E
S

Paraná River

Río de la Plata

Map Key

Mountain
Desert
Rain forest
Grassland
Wetland
Volcano
■ Point of interest
" Waterfall

Laguna del Carbón
Lowest point in South America

Strait of Magellan

Falkland Islands

0   600 miles

0   900 kilometers

SOUTH AMERICA

Many religious festivals take place all over South America. Here, a girl is dancing as she celebrates a Catholic fiesta.

This statue was carved from stone during the Tiwanaku civilization. These people lived long ago near Lake Titicaca in Bolivia.

COUNTRIES South America has just 12 countries—French Guiana is not a country because it belongs to France. All but two of these countries border an ocean. Can you find these two landlocked countries on the map?

CITIES Most of the largest cities are near the oceans. São Paulo, in Brazil, is South America's most populous city. Bolivia has two capital cities: La Paz and Sucre.

PEOPLE The earliest people came from the north long ago. Colonists came from Europe, especially from Spain and Portugal. They brought African slaves to work in the fields. Most people in South America are descendants of these three groups.

LANGUAGES Spanish and Portuguese are the continent's chief languages. Native people speak Quechua or other native languages.

This man plays his guitar to entertain people on the streets of Buenos Aires, in Argentina. Guitar music is popular in South America.

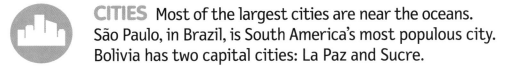

These unpolished stones are emeralds. Colombia is the top producer of these gems.

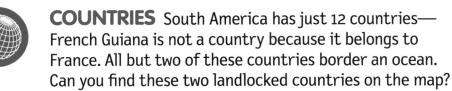

Soccer is the most popular sport in South America. This player from Brazil is focused on scoring a goal.

NORTH AMERICA

Lake Maracaibo
⊛ Caracas
Orinoco River

V E N E Z U E L A

Medellín.

⊛ Bogotá

Cali. **C O L O M B I A**

⊛ Georgetown
⊛ Paramaribo
French Guiana (France)

GUYANA

SURINAME

ATLANTIC OCEAN

⊛ Quito
ECUADOR
.Guayaquil

Negro River
Manaus.
Amazon River
Marajó Island
.Belém

Amazon River

.Fortaleza

P E R U

B R A Z I L

Lima⊛

São Francisco River

Recife.

B O L I V I A
Lake Titicaca
⊛ La Paz

⊛ Sucre

.Salvador

⊛ Brasília

Paraguay River

Paraná River

.Belo Horizonte

PACIFIC OCEAN

P A R A G U A Y

São Paulo.
.Rio de Janeiro

Asunción⊛
—Itaipú Dam

Paraná River

.Porto Alegre

URUGUAY

Santiago⊛

A R G E N T I N A

Buenos Aires⊛
Montevideo⊛

C H I L E

Map Key
- ⊛ Country capital
- • City
- — Dam

Falkland Islands (Islas Malvinas) (U.K.)

0 ___ 600 miles
0 ___ 900 kilometers

The Itaipú Dam, located on the Paraná River between Brazil and Paraguay, is one of the largest hydroelectric dams in the world.

EUROPE

Travel through the countryside in Europe and you're likely to see castles, cuckoo clocks, and cobblestone streets. But Europe is also one of the most modern continents. You can ride one of the world's fastest trains through a tunnel beneath the English Channel, watch sports cars being made in Italy, and visit famous landmarks, such as the Eiffel Tower, in Paris. On a map, Europe may look as if it is part of Asia, but it is considered to be a separate continent.

Most puffins live in the North Atlantic Ocean near Europe, especially in the waters around Iceland. They rely on a diet of small fish.

The warm glow of sunrise lights up Hungary's Parliament Building on the bank of the Danube River in Budapest.

Iceland

Farmland covers much of Europe. Fields of lavender grow in the mild climate east of the Rhône River. Perfume is made from these flowers.

LAND REGIONS Europe's most obvious feature is its long coastline, cut with bays and peninsulas of every size. The Alps are high mountains that form a chain across a large part of southern Europe.

WATER Several large rivers flow across Europe. Some of the most important are the Danube, Rhine, and Volga.

CLIMATE Warm winds from the Atlantic Ocean help give much of Europe a mild, rainy climate. This climate makes parts of Europe good for farming.

PLANTS Europe's largest forests are in the north. Cork and olive trees grow near the Mediterranean Sea.

ANIMALS Reindeer are common in the far north. Many kinds of goatlike animals live in the Alps. Robins, nightingales, and sparrows are among Europe's native birds.

ATLANTIC OCEAN

Ireland

Great Britain

People often try to climb the Matterhorn. It is one of the highest peaks in the Alps.

This is a kind of wild goat called an ibex. It is one of many kinds of hooved animals that live in the Alps and other mountainous parts of the continent.

Europe has many sandy beaches on the Mediterranean Sea. Some of the most famous are along the coasts of Italy, France, and Spain.

PYRENEES

IBERIAN PENINSULA

M e

AFRICA

N

Norwegian Sea

SCANDINAVIAN PENINSULA

URAL MTS.

ASIA

Volga River

North Sea

Baltic Sea

NORTHERN EUROPEAN PLAIN

EUROPE-ASIA BOUNDARY

Caspian Sea Lowest point in Europe

Rhine River

CARPATHIAN MTS.

THE STEPPES

El'brus Highest point in Europe

Caspian Sea

Rhône River

ALPS

Matterhorn

Danube River

CAUCASUS MTS.

APENNINES

BALKAN MTS.

Black Sea

Map Key

ASIA

Sicily

Mount Etna

Crete

Cyprus

Mediterranean Sea

Mountain	
Desert	
Coniferous forest	
Deciduous forest	
Grassland	
Wetland	
Tundra	
Volcano	
——	Europe-Asia boundary

European rabbits live all over the continent.

0	600 miles
0	900 kilometers

COUNTRIES Europe has 46 countries. Even though most of Russia is in Asia (see pages 42–43), it is usually counted as part of Europe because most of its people live there. Vatican City, Europe's smallest country, lies within the city of Rome, Italy. There are five island countries: Iceland, the United Kingdom, Ireland, Malta, and Cyprus.

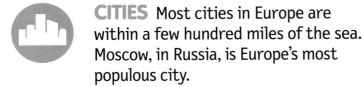

CITIES Most cities in Europe are within a few hundred miles of the sea. Moscow, in Russia, is Europe's most populous city.

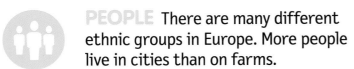

PEOPLE There are many different ethnic groups in Europe. More people live in cities than on farms.

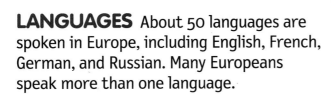

LANGUAGES About 50 languages are spoken in Europe, including English, French, German, and Russian. Many Europeans speak more than one language.

The Colosseum lights up as the sun begins to set in Rome, Italy. This amphitheater was built by the Roman Empire almost 2,000 years ago.

These girls are dressed for a festival in Spain. Such celebrations keep folk traditions alive.

A merchant sells cheese in a market in Ghent, Belgium. Europe is famous for its many kinds of cheese.

The euro is currently the official money in Greece and 18 other member countries of the European Union (see page 61).

Bagpipe music is popular in Scotland, which was once an independent country. Today, Scotland is part of the United Kingdom.

Reykjavík ☀ **ICELAND**

Faroe Islands
(Denmark)

ATLANTIC

OCEAN

Orkney Islands

IRELAND **UNITED**
Dublin ☀ **KINGDOM**

London ☀

English Channel

Paris ☀

F R A

•Bordeaux

PORTUGAL **ANDORRA**

☀ **Madrid**

Lisbon ☀ **S P A I N**

•Seville

Balearic Islands
(Spain)

Gibraltar
(U.K.)

N

Norwegian Sea

Map Key
⊛ Country capital
• City
☐ Disputed territory

0   600 miles
0   900 kilometers

ASIA

EUROPE-ASIA BOUNDARY

Shetland Islands

N O R W A Y
S W E D E N
F I N L A N D

Helsinki ⊛
• St. Petersburg
Oslo ⊛
⊛ Tallinn
Stockholm ⊛
ESTONIA

R U S S I A

Baltic Sea

North Sea

DENMARK
Copenhagen ⊛

LATVIA
Riga ⊛
LITHUANIA
⊛ Vilnius
Kaliningrad (Russia)
• Minsk ⊛
BELARUS

⊛ Moscow

Volga River

KAZAKHSTAN

Volgograd •

NETHERLANDS
• Hamburg
⊛ Amsterdam
⊛ The Hague
Brussels •
Berlin ⊛
Warsaw ⊛
GERMANY
POLAND
BELGIUM
Rhine River

LUXEMBOURG
Prague ⊛
CZECHIA (CZECH REPUBLIC)
Danube River

• Cracow

⊛ Kiev

U K R A I N E

SLOVAKIA
NCE
Vienna ⊛ ⊛ Bratislava
MOLDOVA
Bern ⊛
LIECHTENSTEIN
⊛ Budapest
Chisinau ⊛
SWITZERLAND
AUSTRIA
HUNGARY
Rhône R.
SLOVENIA
Ljubljana ⊛ ⊛ Zagreb
ROMANIA
Crimea

GEORGIA
Tbilisi ⊛
Baku ⊛

CROATIA
Belgrade ⊛
SAN MARINO
BOSNIA AND HERZEGOVINA
Sarajevo •
SERBIA
Danube River
⊛ Bucharest

Black Sea

MONACO
ITALY
MONTENEGRO
KOSOVO
Pristina ⊛
⊛ Sofia
BULGARIA

AZERBAIJAN

Caspian Sea

Corsica (France)
VATICAN CITY
⊛ Rome
Podgorica ⊛
Tirana ⊛
⊛ Skopje
MACEDONIA

NOTE: The countries of Turkey, Georgia, Azerbaijan, Kazakhstan, and Russia are in both Europe and Asia.

ASIA

Sardinia (Italy)
• Naples
ALBANIA
G R E E C E
T
• Istanbul
⊛ Ankara

Mediterranean Sea

Sicily

U R K E Y

⊛ Athens
Valletta ⊛
MALTA

Crete

CYPRUS
⊛ Nicosia

St. Basil's is a famous Russian Orthodox church. It is in Moscow, Russia's capital city.

▶

AFRICA

ASIA

Asia is Earth's largest continent. Mount Everest, the world's highest mountain, is here. Asia also has some of the world's longest rivers, biggest deserts, and thickest forests. The Dead Sea is the lowest place on the continent. It is called "dead" because its water is too salty for fish and other animals to live in. More people live in Asia than anywhere else. The world's very first cities were built in river valleys in Asia long, long ago.

This endangered tiger lives in a forest reserve in India, a country where the number of tigers in the wild has been increasing in recent years.

Bright lights, colorful signs, and bustling crowds are typical of Tokyo, Japan, the most populous city in the world.

THE LAND
ASIA

A climber stands at the top of a peak in the Himalaya. Mount Everest rises in the distance.

LAND REGIONS Much of Asia is a rolling plain covered by grasslands, forests, and tundra. The Himalaya and other high mountains stretch across the south. Deserts cover much of southwestern and central Asia.

WATER Asia has huge rivers and lakes. The Yangtze is the longest river. The Caspian Sea (partly in Europe) is the world's largest saltwater lake. Lake Baikal is the world's deepest lake.

CLIMATE Northern Asia has long, cold winters and short, cool summers. Most of southern Asia is warm year-round with heavy summer rains.

PLANTS Areas of coniferous forest called taiga stretch across the north. The central grasslands are known as the steppes. Rain forests grow in the southeast.

ANIMALS Tigers, giant pandas, and cobras live in the wild only in Asia.

A dromedary, or one-hump, camel walks across the vast desert of the Arabian Peninsula. Camels can carry heavy loads across the desert, are a source of food, and provide hair for weaving cloth.

Mediterranean Sea

Black Sea

CAUCASUS MTS.

Euphrates River

Tigris River

Dead Sea
Lowest point in Asia

Persian Gulf

AFRICA

ARABIAN PENINSULA

EQUATOR

The Three Gorges Dam helps to manage flooding along China's Yangtze River.

N

ARCTIC OCEAN

Bering Sea

EUROPE

EUROPE-ASIA BOUNDARY

URAL MOUNTAINS

Ob River

Irtysh River

Yenisey River

Lena River

Amur River

THE STEPPES

Aral Sea

Caspian Sea

Lake Baikal
Deepest lake in the world

TIAN SHAN

GOBI

Yellow River

PACIFIC OCEAN

Indus River

H I M A L A Y A

Brahmaputra River

Yangtze River

Ganges River

Mt. Everest
Highest point in Asia

Mekong River

Arabian Sea

Bay of Bengal

South China Sea

New Guinea

Trees tower over a native village along a river in eastern Borneo. Rain forests thrive in Indonesia's warm temperatures and abundant rainfall.

| 0 | 600 miles |
| 0 | 900 kilometers |

Map Key

- Mountain
- Desert
- Coniferous forest
- Deciduous forest
- Rain forest
- Grassland
- Wetland
- Tundra
- Volcano
- Dry salt lake
- — Europe-Asia boundary

Sumatra

Borneo

A herder leads his reindeer through the snow in northern Asia. Winters there are cold and last six to seven months.

INDIAN OCEAN

Giant pandas live in the wild only in leafy bamboo forests that grow on mountains in southwestern China.

These are the Petronas Towers in Kuala Lumpur, Malaysia. They are the tallest twin buildings in the world.

EUROPE

RUSSIA

Baltic

NOTE: The countries of Russia, Kazakhstan, Azerbaijan, Georgia, and Turkey are in both Europe and Asia.

Black Sea

Istanbul

Ankara ⊛

TURKEY

GEORGIA

Tbilisi ⊛

ARMENIA

Yerevan ⊛

AZERBAIJAN

LEBANON

Beirut ⊛

SYRIA

Jerusalem ⊛ ⊛ Damascus

ISRAEL ⊛ ⊛ Amman

JORDAN

Baghdad ⊛ Tehran ⊛

IRAQ

I R

KUWAIT ⊛ Kuwait City

SAUDI ARABIA

BAHRAIN

Persian Gulf

Riyadh ⊛

QATAR ⊛

Doha

Abu Dhabi ⊛

UNITED ARAB EMIRATES

AFRICA

Mediterranean Sea

Sanaa ⊛

YEMEN

OMAN

COUNTRIES Asia has 46 countries. China is the largest country with boundaries entirely in Asia. Russia takes up the most area, but it is counted as part of Europe (see pages 36–37). Indonesia is Asia's largest island country.

CITIES Much of Asia is too high, too dry, or too cold for people to live in. Most cities are near the coast or along busy rivers. Tokyo, in Japan, is the most populous city.

PEOPLE Asia has more people than any other continent. Each ethnic group has its own language, customs, and appearance. Many people are farmers, but others work in high-tech industries.

LANGUAGES More than 2,300 languages are spoken by the people of Asia—the most of any continent. Chinese has more native speakers than any other language.

This young boy works in a spice market. In India people mix lots of spices together to make a strong flavor called curry.

This masked dancer is from Bali, one of more than 3,000 islands that make up the country of Indonesia.

This boy in Shanghai, China, draws symbols used in writing the Chinese language. Each symbol stands for a word or an idea.

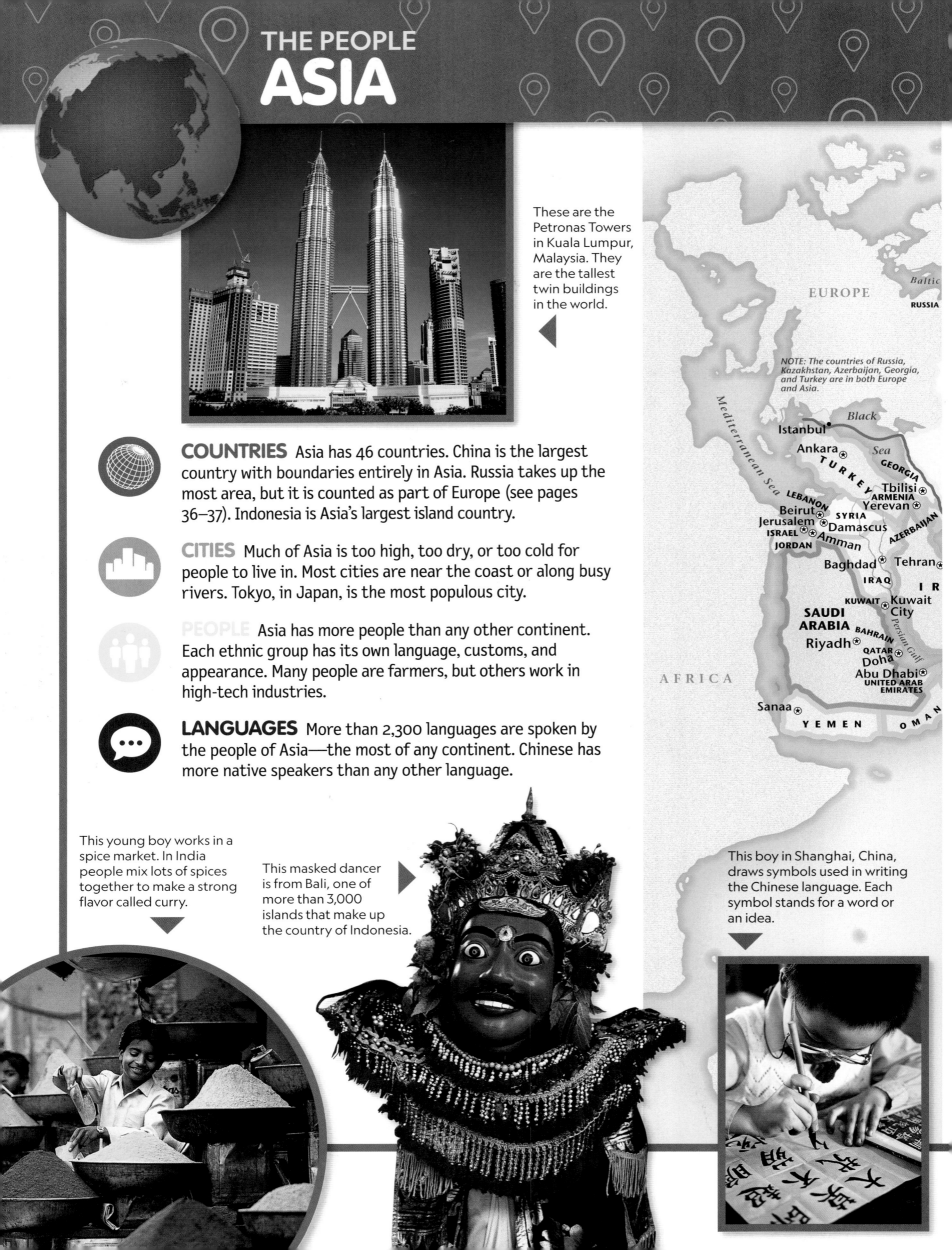

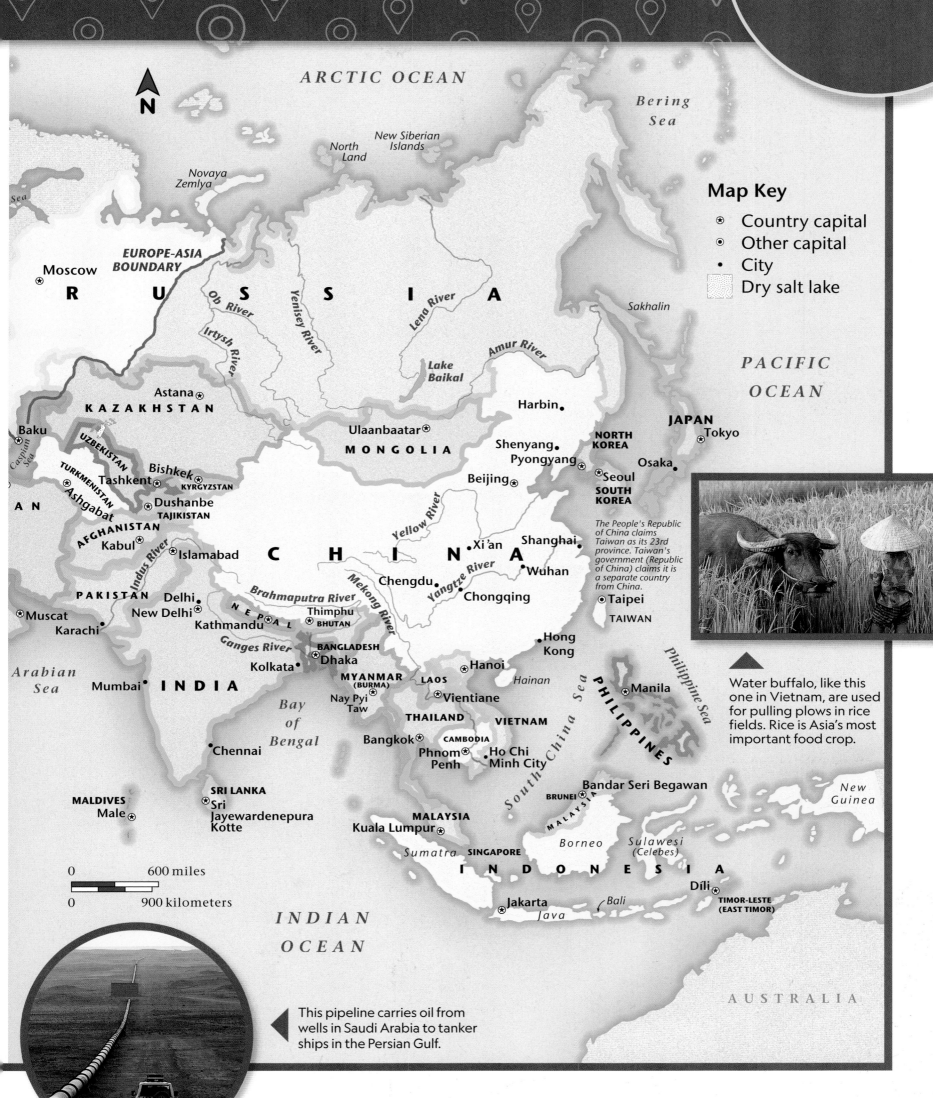

ARCTIC OCEAN

Bering Sea

North Land

New Siberian Islands

Novaya Zemlya

N

Sea

Map Key

⊛ Country capital
◉ Other capital
• City
▨ Dry salt lake

• Moscow

R U S S I A

Ob River

Yenisey River

Irtysh River

Lena River

Amur River

Lake Baikal

Sakhalin

PACIFIC OCEAN

• Astana ⊛

K A Z A K H S T A N

• Ulaanbaatar ⊛

M O N G O L I A

• Harbin

JAPAN

Tokyo ⊛

• Baku

UZBEKISTAN

Caspian Sea

• Shenyang

NORTH KOREA

Pyongyang ⊛

Osaka •

TURKMENISTAN

Bishkek ⊛

Tashkent •

KYRGYZSTAN

⊛ Seoul

• Beijing ⊛

SOUTH KOREA

AN

• Ashgabat ⊛

Dushanbe ⊛

TAJIKISTAN

AFGHANISTAN

Kabul ⊛

C H I N A

Yellow River

• Xi'an

• Shanghai

The People's Republic of China claims Taiwan as its 23rd province. Taiwan's government (Republic of China) claims it is a separate country from China.

Islamabad ⊛

Indus River

Chengdu •

• Wuhan

Yangtze River

PAKISTAN

Delhi •

New Delhi ⊛

Brahmaputra River

Mekong River

• Chongqing

◉ Taipei

TAIWAN

Muscat ⊛

N E P A L

Thimphu ⊛

Karachi •

Kathmandu ⊛

BHUTAN

Hong Kong

Ganges River

BANGLADESH

Kolkata •

Dhaka ⊛

• Hanoi ⊛

Arabian Sea

I N D I A

MYANMAR (BURMA)

LAOS

Hainan

• Manila ⊛

Mumbai •

Nay Pyi Taw ⊛

Vientiane ⊛

Philippine Sea

Bay of Bengal

THAILAND

VIETNAM

P H I L I P P I N E S

• Chennai

Bangkok ⊛

CAMBODIA

Phnom Penh ⊛

• Ho Chi Minh City

South China Sea

SRI LANKA

MALDIVES

Sri Jayewardenepura Kotte ◉

Bandar Seri Begawan ⊛

BRUNEI

New Guinea

Male ⊛

MALAYSIA

Kuala Lumpur ⊛

MALAYSIA

Borneo

Sulawesi (Celebes)

0 ———— 600 miles

0 ———— 900 kilometers

Sumatra

SINGAPORE

I N D O N E S I A

Jakarta ⊛

Java

Bali

Díli ◉

TIMOR-LESTE (EAST TIMOR)

INDIAN OCEAN

AUSTRALIA

▶ Water buffalo, like this one in Vietnam, are used for pulling plows in rice fields. Rice is Asia's most important food crop.

◀ This pipeline carries oil from wells in Saudi Arabia to tanker ships in the Persian Gulf.

EUROPE-ASIA BOUNDARY

AFRICA

Elephants, lions, gorillas, hippopotamuses, giraffes, and zebras are among the amazing animals you can see in Africa's parks, plains, forests, and mountains. You can also visit a busy, modern city such as Nairobi, in Kenya; shop in colorful, outdoor markets; and see how diamonds are mined in South Africa. You can even take a sailboat ride past ancient temples along the Nile and climb some of the world's highest sand dunes in Earth's biggest hot desert—the Sahara.

African elephants roam the continent's grasslands. They are Earth's largest land animal.

Buildings in Ouarzazate, Morocco, are an example of the traditional Arab architecture found in northern Africa.

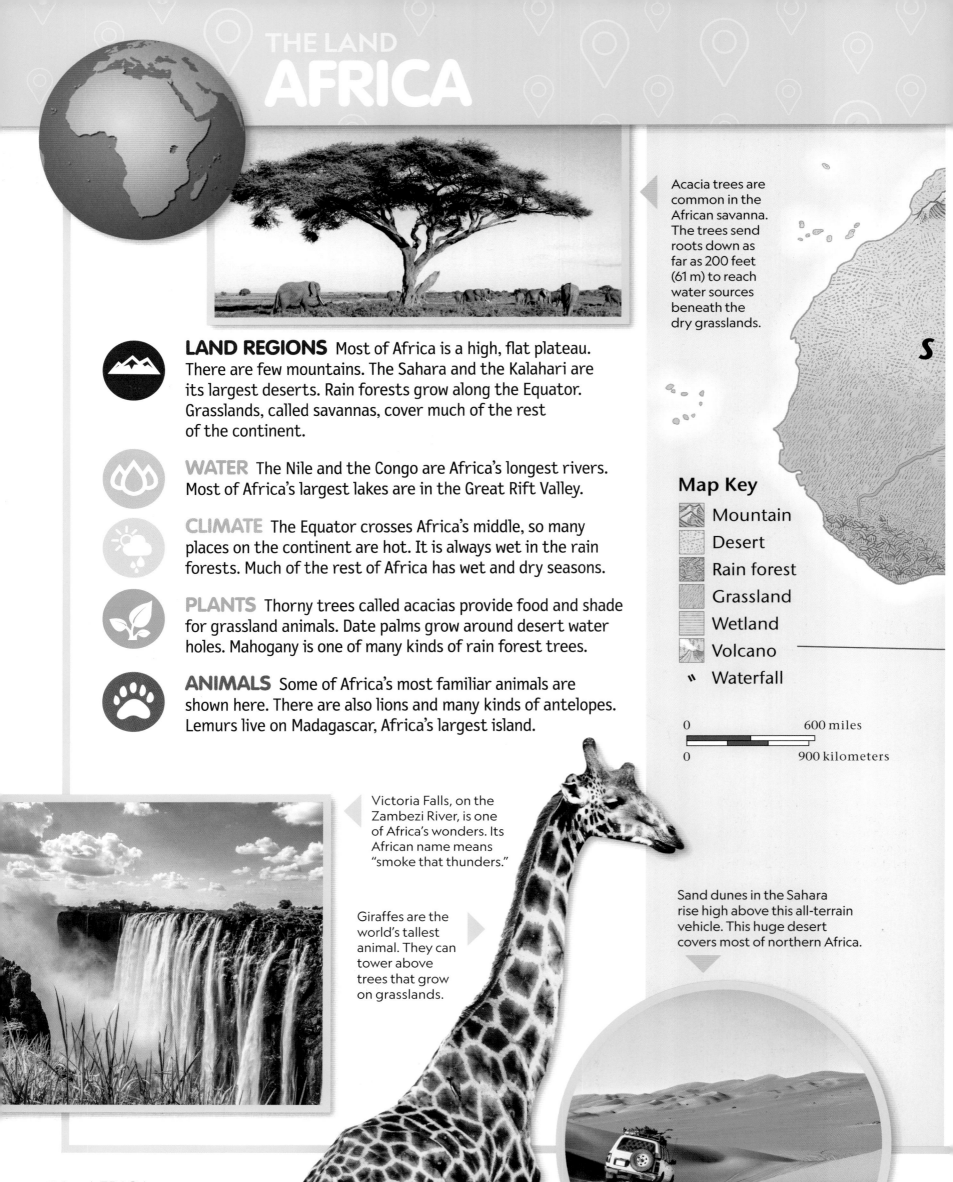

THE LAND
AFRICA

Acacia trees are common in the African savanna. The trees send roots down as far as 200 feet (61 m) to reach water sources beneath the dry grasslands.

LAND REGIONS Most of Africa is a high, flat plateau. There are few mountains. The Sahara and the Kalahari are its largest deserts. Rain forests grow along the Equator. Grasslands, called savannas, cover much of the rest of the continent.

WATER The Nile and the Congo are Africa's longest rivers. Most of Africa's largest lakes are in the Great Rift Valley.

CLIMATE The Equator crosses Africa's middle, so many places on the continent are hot. It is always wet in the rain forests. Much of the rest of Africa has wet and dry seasons.

PLANTS Thorny trees called acacias provide food and shade for grassland animals. Date palms grow around desert water holes. Mahogany is one of many kinds of rain forest trees.

ANIMALS Some of Africa's most familiar animals are shown here. There are also lions and many kinds of antelopes. Lemurs live on Madagascar, Africa's largest island.

Map Key

- Mountain
- Desert
- Rain forest
- Grassland
- Wetland
- Volcano
- " Waterfall

| 0 | 600 miles |
| 0 | 900 kilometers |

Victoria Falls, on the Zambezi River, is one of Africa's wonders. Its African name means "smoke that thunders."

Giraffes are the world's tallest animal. They can tower above trees that grow on grasslands.

Sand dunes in the Sahara rise high above this all-terrain vehicle. This huge desert covers most of northern Africa.

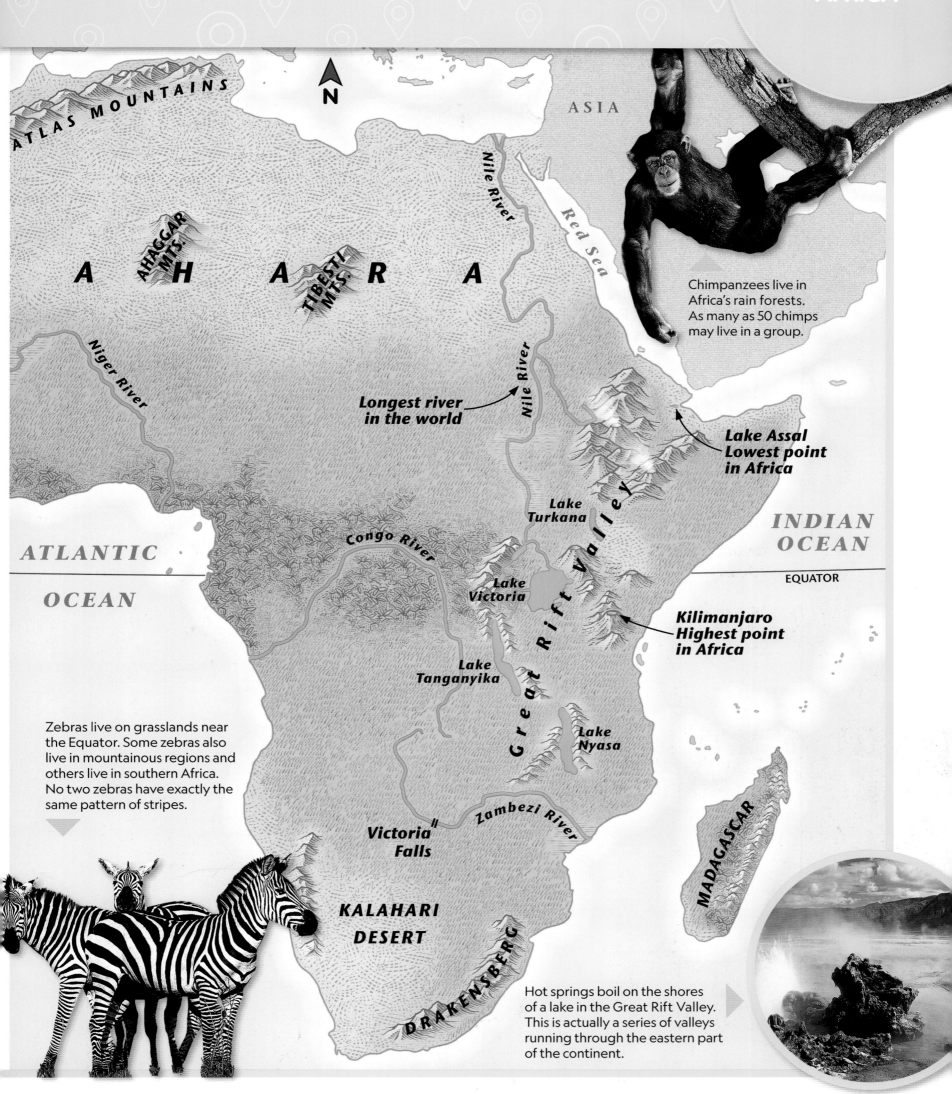

ATLAS MOUNTAINS

ASIA

N

S A H A R A

AHAGGAR MTS.

TIBESTI MTS.

Nile River

Red Sea

Niger River

Nile River

Longest river in the world

Chimpanzees live in Africa's rain forests. As many as 50 chimps may live in a group.

Lake Assal Lowest point in Africa

Lake Turkana

Congo River

Great Rift Valley

INDIAN OCEAN

ATLANTIC

Lake Victoria

EQUATOR

OCEAN

Kilimanjaro Highest point in Africa

Lake Tanganyika

Zebras live on grasslands near the Equator. Some zebras also live in mountainous regions and others live in southern Africa. No two zebras have exactly the same pattern of stripes.

Lake Nyasa

MADAGASCAR

Zambezi River

Victoria Falls

KALAHARI DESERT

DRAKENSBERG

Hot springs boil on the shores of a lake in the Great Rift Valley. This is actually a series of valleys running through the eastern part of the continent.

Small sailboats called feluccas carry trade goods along the Nile. The river flows north out of Lake Victoria.

Casablanca

Canary Islands (Spain)

WESTERN SAHARA (Morocco)

MAURITANIA

Nouakchott ✶
CABO VERDE
✶ **Praia**   **Dakar**   SENEGAL
Banjul ✶   **Bamako** ✶
GAMBIA   **GUINEA-**
Bissau ✶ **BISSAU**
GUINEA
Conakry ✶ **Yamoussoukro** ✶
Freetown ✶
SIERRA LEONE   LIBERIA
Monrovia ✶
CÔTE D'IVOIRE (IVORY COAST)

COUNTRIES Much of Africa was ruled by European countries from the late 1800s to the mid 1900s. Today, there are 54 independent countries. Algeria has the most land. Nigeria has the most people.

CITIES Cairo and Lagos are Africa's most populous cities. Both are busy port cities and centers of trade. But many people live in villages and on farms rather than in cities.

PEOPLE Most people in northern Africa are Arabic-speaking Muslims. Most black Africans living south of the Sahara belong to hundreds of different ethnic groups. Many Europeans live in major cities and in South Africa.

LANGUAGES Arabic is spoken in northern Africa. Native languages are spoken south of the Sahara. English, French, and Portuguese are the main European languages.

These students in Kenya study many of the same subjects you do. Their classes are taught in English.

These boys are picking dates. Algeria is a leading producer of this fruit.

The Sphinx and the pyramid behind it were built by people who lived in Egypt thousands of years ago.

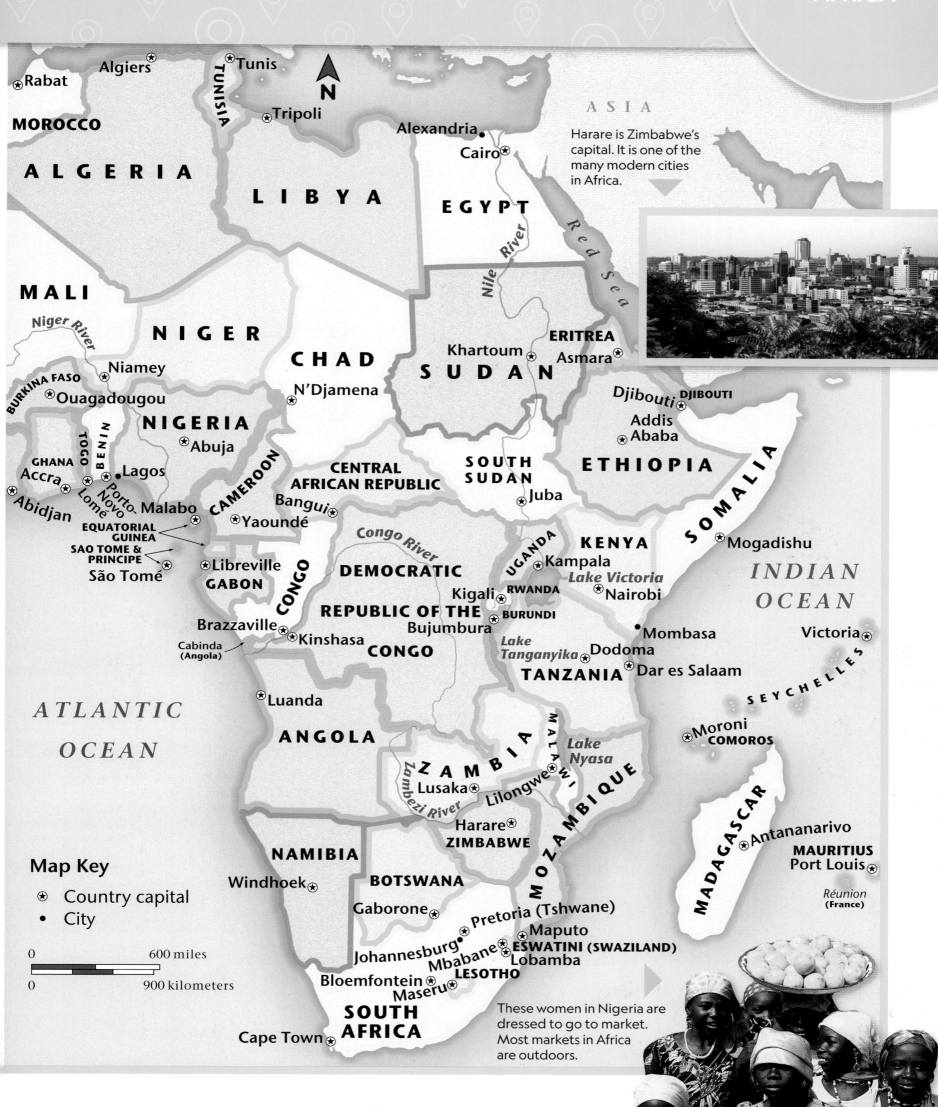

Rabat

Algiers

Tunis

TUNISIA

N

Tripoli

Alexandria

Cairo

ASIA

Harare is Zimbabwe's capital. It is one of the many modern cities in Africa.

MOROCCO

ALGERIA

LIBYA

EGYPT

Nile River

Red Sea

MALI

NIGER

CHAD

Khartoum

SUDAN

ERITREA

Asmara

Niger River

Niamey

N'Djamena

Djibouti DJIBOUTI

BURKINA FASO

Ouagadougou

NIGERIA

Abuja

CENTRAL AFRICAN REPUBLIC

SOUTH SUDAN

Addis Ababa

ETHIOPIA

TOGO

BENIN

GHANA

Accra

Lagos

Juba

Abidjan

Lomé

Porto Novo

Malabo

CAMEROON

Bangui

SOMALIA

EQUATORIAL GUINEA

Yaoundé

Mogadishu

SAO TOME & PRINCIPE

Libreville

Congo River

DEMOCRATIC

UGANDA

KENYA

São Tomé

GABON

CONGO

REPUBLIC OF THE

Kampala

Lake Victoria

Kigali RWANDA

Nairobi

INDIAN OCEAN

Brazzaville

Kinshasa

BURUNDI

Bujumbura

CONGO

Lake Tanganyika

Dodoma

Mombasa

Victoria

Cabinda (Angola)

TANZANIA

Dar es Salaam

SEYCHELLES

Luanda

Moroni COMOROS

ATLANTIC OCEAN

ANGOLA

ZAMBIA

MALAWI

Lake Nyasa

Zambezi River

Lusaka

Lilongwe

MOZAMBIQUE

MADAGASCAR

Antananarivo

MAURITIUS

Port Louis

Harare

ZIMBABWE

NAMIBIA

Réunion (France)

Map Key

⊛ Country capital

• City

BOTSWANA

Windhoek

Gaborone

Pretoria (Tshwane)

Maputo

0   600 miles

Johannesburg

Mbabane

ESWATINI (SWAZILAND)

Lobamba

0   900 kilometers

Bloemfontein

LESOTHO

Maseru

SOUTH AFRICA

These women in Nigeria are dressed to go to market. Most markets in Africa are outdoors.

Cape Town

AUSTRALIA

Australia is an unusual place. It is Earth's smallest and flattest continent and one of the driest, too. "Aussies," as Australians refer to themselves, call their continent the "land down under" because the entire continent lies south of, or "under," the Equator. Most Australians live in cities along the coast. But Australia also has huge cattle and sheep ranches. Many ranch children live far from school. They get their lessons by mail or from the internet. Their doctors even visit by airplane!

Kangaroos live in the wild only in Australia. They live in groups called mobs.

The Sydney Opera House is recognized worldwide for its unique design.

THE LAND
AUSTRALIA

The "Three Sisters" rock formation is a stunning site in the Blue Mountains of Australia. These mountains are part of the Great Dividing Range.

INDIAN OCEAN

A sign warns drivers to look out for kangaroos. The red rock formation, called Uluru by Aboriginals and Ayers Rock by others, is in the Western Plateau.

 LAND REGIONS The Great Dividing Range stretches through eastern Australia and into Tasmania. Most of the rest of Australia is a plateau covered by grasslands and deserts.

 WATER The Darling, Australia's longest river, is dry during part of the year. So is Lake Eyre, the continent's largest lake. Water lies underground in the Great Artesian Basin.

 CLIMATE Much of the continent is very dry. Winds called monsoons bring heavy seasonal rains to the northern coast. Southern Australia can be cold in winter, but much of the continent is warm year-round.

 PLANTS Eucalyptus, or gum, trees and acacias are the most common kinds of plants. They grow throughout much of Australia.

ANIMALS Australia has many unusual mammals. Female koalas and kangaroos raise their young in pouches on their bellies. The platypus is a mammal that has a bill like a duck's. Its babies hatch from eggs.

Moss covers trees and logs in a forest in Tasmania. This island has a much wetter climate than most of mainland Australia.

The cackling laugh of the kookaburra is a familiar forest sound.

Hamersley Range

Darling Range

Map Key

- Mountain
- Desert
- Deciduous forest
- Rain forest
- Grassland
- Wetland
- Dry salt lake
- Reef
- ■ Point of interest

Coral Sea

Gulf of Carpentaria

Kimberley Plateau

Longest coral reef system in the world

Great Barrier Reef

W E S T E R N

MacDonnell Ranges

P L A T E A U

G R E A T

A R T E S I A N

■ Uluru (Ayers Rock)

B A S I N

G R E A T   D I V I D I N G   R A N G E

Lake Eyre Lowest point in Australia

Flinders Ranges

Darling River

Mt. Kosciuszko Highest point in Australia

Murray River

Great Australian Bight

Limestone towers rise above a desert in Western Australia. Desert covers much of the continent.

Bass Strait

Koalas live only in eucalyptus trees. At one time koalas almost became extinct. Now they are protected by strict laws.

Tasmania

| 0 | | | 600 miles |
| 0 | | | 900 kilometers |

AUSTRALIA

Surfing is popular in Australia. There is even a suburb of Queensland's Gold Coast named Surfers Paradise.

INDIAN OCEAN

• Port Hedland

WESTERN AUSTRALIA

COUNTRIES Australia is the only continent that is also a country. It is divided into six states plus the Northern and Australian Capital territories.

CITIES All the chief cities are near the coast except the capital, Canberra, which is almost 100 miles (160 km) inland. Sydney has the most people, followed by Melbourne, Brisbane, and Perth.

PEOPLE Most Australians are descendants of settlers from the United Kingdom and Ireland. Aboriginals came to Australia from Asia some 40,000 years ago.

LANGUAGES English is the main language of Australia. Aboriginals speak some 250 different languages.

⦿ Perth

The world's largest cultured pearls are grown in oyster beds along Australia's northern coast.

Cafés can be hundreds of miles apart in the outback, a dry, remote, and largely uninhabited region.

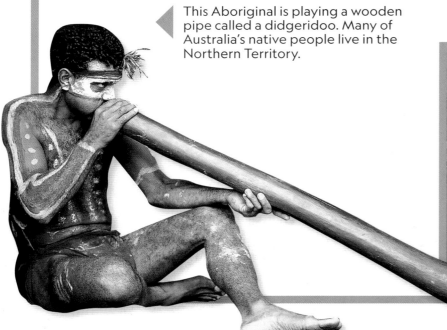

This Aboriginal is playing a wooden pipe called a didgeridoo. Many of Australia's native people live in the Northern Territory.

N

Darwin

Gulf of Carpentaria

NORTHERN TERRITORY

Cairns

Townsville

Mount Isa

QUEENSLAND

Mackay

Alice Springs

A U S T R A L I A

Rockhampton

SOUTH AUSTRALIA

Lake Eyre

Huge cattle farms are called stations. Some of the largest are in Western Australia.

Brisbane

Gold Coast

Darling River

NEW SOUTH WALES

Great Australian Bight

Adelaide

KANGAROO I.

Murray River

Sydney

Canberra

AUSTRALIAN CAPITAL TERRITORY

VICTORIA

Melbourne

Map Key
⊛ Country capital
⊙ State or territory capital
• City
▦ Dry salt lake

TASMANIA

Hobart

0   600 miles
0   900 kilometers

Each year in September, the Brisbane Festival attracts more than a million people to an almost monthlong arts and culture program that includes music, dance, and theater.

ANTARCTICA

*B*rrrr! Antarctica takes first place as the coldest continent. It is the land around the South Pole. An ice sheet two miles (3 km) thick in places covers most of the land. Temperatures rarely get above freezing. It is also the only continent that has no countries. It has research stations but no cities. The only people are scientists, explorers, and tourists. Everyone stays for a while, then goes home. The largest land animals that live here year-round are a few kinds of insects!

Antarctica's deep-diving Weddell seals can stay underwater 45 minutes as they hunt for fish.

Water temperatures around Antarctica range from 28°F to 50°F (-2°C to 10°C). Whales and other sea animals inhabit these cold waters all or part of each year.

This strong-sided ship is an icebreaker. It cuts a path through ice in the Ross Sea.

ATLANTIC OCEAN

ANTARCTIC CIRCLE

ANTARCTIC

⛰ LAND REGIONS
The Transantarctic Mountains divide the continent into two parts. East Antarctica, where the South Pole is located, is mostly a high, flat, icy area. West Antarctica is mountainous. The Antarctic Peninsula extends like a finger toward South America. Vinson Massif is the highest peak.

Scientists, including those at Argentina's Brown Station, spend months studying changes in Earth's environment.

💧 WATER
Most of Earth's freshwater is frozen in Antarctica's ice sheet. The ice breaks off when it meets the sea. These huge floating chunks of ice in the ocean are called icebergs.

☀ CLIMATE
Antarctica is cold, windy, and dry. What little snow falls turns to ice. The thick ice sheet has built up over millions of years.

Bellingshausen Sea

ELLSWORTH LAND

Amundsen Sea

🌱 PLANTS
Billions of tiny plants live in the surrounding oceans. Mosses and lichens grow on exposed rocks.

🐾 ANIMALS
Penguins and other seabirds nest on the coast. Whales, seals, and tiny shrimplike krill live in the oceans.

Adélie penguins live in large colonies along the shores of Antarctica and nearby islands. They feed mainly on fish and krill.

Jellyfish grow very large under the sea ice around the continent. Here they have few enemies so they live a long time.

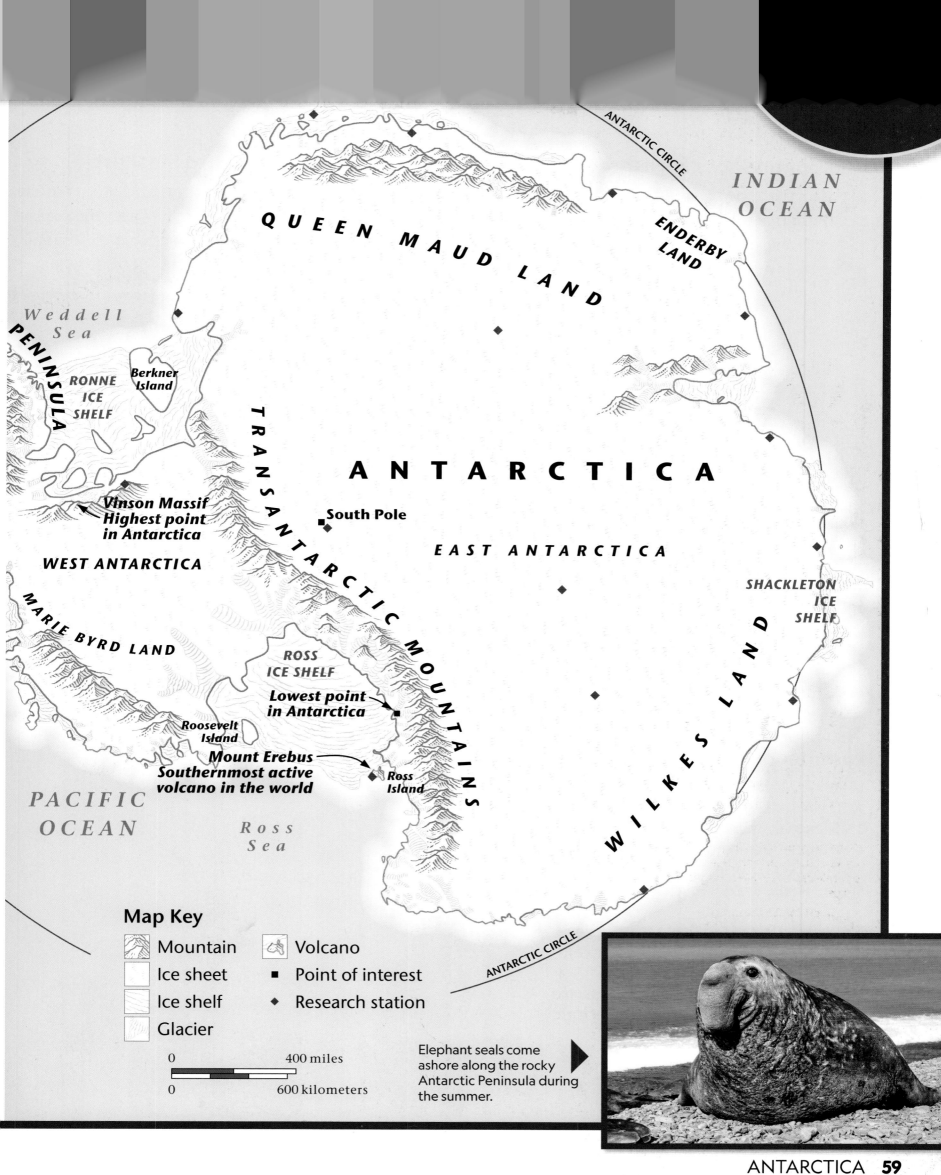

ANTARCTIC CIRCLE

INDIAN OCEAN

ENDERBY LAND

QUEEN MAUD LAND

Weddell Sea

PENINSULA

RONNE ICE SHELF

Berkner Island

TRANSANTARCTIC MOUNTAINS

ANTARCTICA

Vinson Massif Highest point in Antarctica

WEST ANTARCTICA

South Pole

EAST ANTARCTICA

SHACKLETON ICE SHELF

MARIE BYRD LAND

ROSS ICE SHELF

Lowest point in Antarctica

Roosevelt Island

Mount Erebus Southernmost active volcano in the world

Ross Island

WILKES LAND

PACIFIC OCEAN

Ross Sea

ANTARCTIC CIRCLE

Map Key

Mountain

Volcano

Ice sheet

■ Point of interest

Ice shelf

◆ Research station

Glacier

| 0 | 400 miles |
| 0 | 600 kilometers |

Elephant seals come ashore along the rocky Antarctic Peninsula during the summer.

WORLD AT A GLANCE

Land

The Continents, Largest to Smallest

1. **Asia:** 17,208,000 sq mi (44,570,000 sq km)
2. **Africa:** 11,608,000 sq mi (30,065,000 sq km)
3. **North America:** 9,449,000 sq mi (24,474,000 sq km)
4. **South America:** 6,880,000 sq mi (17,819,000 sq km)
5. **Antarctica:** 5,100,000 sq mi (13,209,000 sq km)
6. **Europe:** 3,841,000 sq mi (9,947,000 sq km)
7. **Australia:** 2,989,000 sq mi (7,741,000 sq km)

People

More than 7.5 billion people live on Earth in almost 200 countries. More than half of the world's people live in Asia. A little more than half of the global population lives in towns and cities.

Five Largest Countries by Number of People (2017 data)

1. **China, Asia:** 1,379,303,000 people
2. **India, Asia:** 1,281,936,000 people
3. **United States, North America:** 326,626,000 people
4. **Indonesia, Asia:** 260,581,000 people
5. **Brazil, South America:** 207,353,000 people

Ten Largest Cities* by Number of People (2016 data)

1. **Tokyo, Japan (Asia):** 38,140,000 people
2. **Delhi, India (Asia):** 26,454,000 people
3. **Shanghai, China (Asia):** 24,484,000
4. **Mumbai (Bombay), India (Asia):** 21,357,000 people
5. **São Paulo, Brazil (South America):** 21,297,000 people
6. **Beijing, China (Asia):** 21,240,000 people
7. **Mexico City, Mexico (North America):** 21,157,000 people
8. **Cairo, Egypt (Africa):** 19,128,000 people
9. **New York City, U.S.A. (North America):** 18,604,000 people
10. **Dhaka, Bangladesh (Asia):** 18,237,000 people

*Figures are for metropolitan areas

Water

The Oceans, Largest to Smallest

1. **Pacific Ocean:** 69,000,000 sq mi (178,800,000 sq km)
2. **Atlantic Ocean:** 35,400,000 sq mi (91,700,000 sq km)
3. **Indian Ocean:** 29,400,000 sq mi (76,200,000 sq km)
4. **Arctic Ocean:** 5,600,000 sq mi (14,700,000 sq km)

Highest, Tallest, Longest, Largest

The numbers below show locations on the map.

1 **Highest Mountain on a Continent**
Mt. Everest, in Asia: 29,035 ft (8,850 m)

2 **Tallest Waterfall**
Angel Falls, in South America: 3,212 ft (979 m)

3 **Largest Island**
Greenland, borders the Arctic and Atlantic Oceans: 836,000 sq mi (2,166,000 sq km)

4 **Largest Ocean**
Pacific Ocean: 69,000,000 sq mi (178,800,000 sq km)

5 **Longest River**
Nile River, in Africa: 4,400 mi (7,081 km)

6 **Largest Freshwater Lake**
Lake Superior, in North America: 31,700 sq mi (82,100 sq km)

7 **Largest Saltwater Lake**
Caspian Sea, in Europe-Asia: 143,200 sq mi (371,000 sq km)

8 **Longest Coral Reef System**
Great Barrier Reef, in Australia: 1,429 miles (2,300 km)

9 **Largest Hot Desert**
Sahara, in Africa: 3,475,000 sq mi (9,000,000 sq km)

10 **Largest Cold Desert**
Antarctica: 5,100,000 sq mi (13,209,000 sq km)

GLOSSARY

Arab people living in the Arabian Peninsula of southwestern Asia or in northern Africa who are linked by language and culture

capital city the seat of government for a country, state, or province

city a settled place where people work in jobs other than farming

colonist a person who settles in a new place, often to claim land for another country

coral reef a stony formation in warm, shallow ocean water that is made up of the skeletons of tiny sea animals called corals

country a place that has boundaries, a name, a flag, and a government that is the highest world authority over the land and the people who live there

environment the world around you, including people, cities, plants and animals, air, water—everything

ethnic group people who share a common ancestry, language, beliefs, and traditions

euro the official currency of the European Union

European Union an organization of 28 European countries (Austria,* Belgium,* Bulgaria, Croatia, Cyprus,* Czechia [Czech Republic], Denmark, Estonia,* Finland,* France,* Germany,* Greece,* Hungary, Ireland,* Italy,* Latvia,* Lithuania,* Luxembourg,* Malta,* Netherlands,* Poland, Portugal,* Romania, Slovakia,* Slovenia,* Spain,* Sweden, and United Kingdom) as of July 2018. Countries marked with an asterisk (*) use the euro as their official currency.

glacier a large, slow-moving mass of ice. Glaciers that cover huge areas are called ice sheets, or continental glaciers

hydroelectric a type of electricity made by harnessing the energy of running water

lemur a mammal that is a kind of primate living in the wild only on Madagascar and other nearby African islands. Most kinds of lemurs are endangered.

lichen a plantlike organism that is part alga and part fungus and that usually lives where few plants can survive

mosses nonflowering, low-growing green plants that grow on rocks and trees

Muslim a person who practices Islam, a religion that has more than two billion followers

outback the dry interior region of Australia where few people live

plains large areas of mainly flat land often covered with grasses

plateau a large, mainly level area of high land

province a unit of government similar to a state

state a unit of government that takes up a specific area within a country, as in one of the 50 large political units in the United States

steppe a Russian word for the grasslands that stretch from eastern Europe into Asia

taiga a Russian word for the scattered coniferous forests that grow in cold, northern regions

tributary a river or stream that flows into a larger river

West Indies a chain of islands stretching from the Bahamas to the northern coast of Venezuela that separates the Gulf of Mexico and the Caribbean Sea from the Atlantic Ocean.

METRIC CONVERSIONS FOUND IN THIS ATLAS

CONVERSIONS TO METRIC MEASUREMENTS

WHEN YOU KNOW	MULTIPLY BY	TO FIND
INCHES (IN)	2.54	CENTIMETERS (CM)
FEET (FT)	0.30	METERS (M)
MILES (MI)	1.61	KILOMETERS (KM)
SQUARE MILES (SQ MI)	2.59	SQUARE KILOMETERS (SQ KM)
POUNDS (LB)	0.45	KILOGRAMS (KG)

CONVERSIONS FROM METRIC MEASUREMENTS

WHEN YOU KNOW	MULTIPLY BY	TO FIND
CENTIMETERS (CM)	0.39	INCHES (IN)
METERS (M)	3.28	FEET (FT)
KILOMETERS (KM)	0.62	MILES (MI)
SQUARE KILOMETERS (SQ KM)	0.39	SQUARE MILES (SQ MI)
KILOGRAMS (KG)	2.20	POUNDS (LB)

INDEX

Pictures and the text that describes them have their page numbers printed in **bold** type.

Photo Credits

COVER
(giraffe), jaroslava V/Shutterstock; (Earth), Ragnarock/Shutterstock; (Eiffel Tower), WDG Photo/Shutterstock; (train), scanrail/Shutterstock; (Africa landscape), Graeme Shannon/Shutterstock; (toucan), Eduardo Rivero/Shutterstock; (hot air balloon), topseller/Shutterstock; Cover flap (panda), Eric Isselee/Shutterstock; Back Cover (snowboarder), robcocquyt/Shutterstock; (penguins), Art Wolfe/Getty Images; (jaguar), Steve Winter/National Geographic Image Collection; (elephant), Linettesimoesphotography/Dreamstime; (Sydney Opera House), Nadezda Zavitaeva/Shutterstock; (city), John W Banagan/Getty Images; (windmill), JacobH/Getty Images

FRONT MATTER
2 (UP), Matthew Baker/Getty Images; 2 (LO), Steve Winter/National Geographic Image Collection; 3 (UP LE), AndreyKrav/Getty Images; 3 (CTR LE), ewastudio/Getty Images; 3 (LO), Art Wolfe/Getty Images; 3 (UP RT), JohnCrux/Getty Images; 3 (LO LE), Leonid Andronov/Getty Images; 5, Wavebreakmedia/Getty Images; 8 (UP LE), Jo Ann Snover/Shutterstock; 8 (UP), John Noble; 8 (LO LE), A. Witte/C. Mahaney/Getty Images; 9 (CTR RT), Stuart McCall/Getty Images; 9 (UP RT), Martine Mouchy; 9 (LO), Mark Harris/Getty Images; 9 (UP CTR), africa924/Getty Images; 12 (LO LE), John Warden/Getty Images; 12 (RT), Steven Sweinberg/Getty Images; 12 (CTR), Raylight3_Dreamstime; 13 (UP), Will Salter/Getty Images; 13 (UP CTR), jxfzsy/Getty Images; 13 (LO CTR RT), Stephen and Michele Vaughan; 13 (LO LE), Cosmo Condina/Getty Images; 13 (LO CTR), Michael Nichols; 13 (LO RT), Tom Bean/Getty Images

NORTH AMERICA
16, Robert Postma/Design Pics/Getty Images; 16–17, Matthew Baker/Getty Images; 18 (UP RT), Charles Krebs/Getty Images; 18 (UP CTR), Stephen Krasemann/Getty Images; 18 (CTR), Mark Lewis/Getty Images; 18 (LO LE), Bruce Wilson/Getty Images; 18-19 (LO), James Randklev/Getty Images; 19, Tony Craddock/Shutterstock; 20 (UP), robcocquyt/Shutterstock; 20 (UP RT), George Hunter; 20 (LO RT), Fito Pardo/Getty Images; 20 (LO RT), kravka/Shutterstock; 20 (LO LE), pixynook/Getty Images; 20 (LO CTR), Alison Wright/Getty Images; 21, Will & Deni McIntyre/Getty Images; 22 (CTR), Billy Hustace/Getty Images; 22 (LO LE), Jake Rajs/Getty Images; 22 (UP RT), David Young-Wolff/PhotoEdit; 23 (RT), Tommy Larey/Shutterstock; 23 (LO LE), Philip Coblentz/Corbis; 23 (LO RT), Hemis/Alamy; 24 (UP), Tim Thompson; 24 (CTR), Cosmo Condina/Getty Images; 24 (LO LE), Icon Sportswire/Getty Images; 25 (UP), Chris Tomaidis/Getty Images; 25 (LO), Wayne R Bilenduke/Getty Images; 25 (CTR RT), Jody Ann/Shutterstock

SOUTH AMERICA
26, Steve Winter/National Geographic Image Collection; 26–27, Danita Delimont/Getty Images; 28 (LO RT), Nicholas Divore/Getty Images; 28 (LO CTR), James R. Holland; 28 (UP), Bryan Parsley; 28 (LO LE), Frans Lanting; 28 (UP CTR), Nicholas Divore/Getty Images; 30 (UP), Lori Epstein/NG Staff; 30 (UP CTR), Gary Yim/Shutterstock; 30 (LO CTR), RJ Lerich/Shutterstock; 30 (LO LE), Robert Frerk/Getty Images; 30 (LO RT), Don Kincaid/Stars and Stripes; 31 (LO), Mykola Gomeniuk/Shutterstock

EUROPE
32, Sigita Playdon/Getty Images; 32-33, AndreyKrav/Getty Images; 34 (UP), James Balog/Getty Images; 34 (UP), Michael Busselle/Getty Images; 34-0 (LO LE), Jayone1981/Dreamstime; 34 (LO RT), Joseph Sohm-Visions of America/Getty Images; 35 (LO LE), Bruce Coleman Ltd.; 36 (LO RT), Yann Layma/Getty Images; 36 (LO RT), unknown1861/Shutterstock; 36 (CTR), Medio Images/Index Stock Imagery; 36 (CTR), Fotosearch; 36 (CTR), Maarten Udema Photography; 37 (UP), Vladitto/Shutterstock; 37 (UP), Anthony Cassidy/Getty Images

ASIA
38, ewastudio/Getty Images; 38–39, John W. Banagan/Getty Images; 40 (UP), Chris Noble/Getty Images; 40 (LO LE), MLenny/Getty Images; 40 (CTR), Robert Morton/iStockphoto.com; 40 (LO RT), Paul Harris/Getty Images; 41 (UP), Rafal Cichawa/Shutterstock; 41 (LO RT), Keren Su/Getty Images; 42 (LO RT), Michael Ventura; 42 (LO LE), Nicholas DeVore/Getty Images; 42 (LO LE), Kenneth Love; 42 (LO), pistolseven/Shutterstock; 43 (RT), Keren Su/Getty Images; 43 (LO), Wayne Eastep/Getty Images

AFRICA
44–45, Leonid Andronov/Getty Images; 44, Linettesimoesphotography/Dreamstime; 46 (LO LE), PocholoCalapre/Getty Images; 46 (LO RT), PatrickPoendl/Getty Images; 46 (LO CTR), Michael Busselle/Getty Images; 47 (LO LE), Kevin Shafer/Getty Images; 47 (LO RT), Michael Busselle/Getty Images; 47 (UP), Tim Davis; 48 (RT), Art Directors & TRIP/Alamy; 48 (UP), A Rey/Getty Images; 48 (LO), Sylvain Grandadam/Getty Images; 48 (CTR LE), RZAF_Images/Alamy; 49 (UP), Jason Venkatasamy/Alamy; 49 (LO), Sally Mayman/Getty Images

AUSTRALIA
50, JohnCrux/Getty Images; 50–51 (UP CTR), Nadezda Zavitaeva/Shutterstock; 52 (LO CTR), Fred Bavendam; 52 (UP CTR), Nic Cleave Photography/Alamy; 52 (LO RT), Andrew Chin/Shutterstock; 52 (UP), Wouter Tolenaars/Shutterstock; 53 (UP), Jason Edwards/National Geographic Image Collection; 53 (LO LE), Penny Tweedie/Getty Images; 54 (UP CTR), Myfanwy Jane Webb/iStockphoto.com; 54 (LO RT), Oliver Strewe/Getty Images; 54 (UP), David Doubilet; 54 (LO LE), Paul Souders/Getty Images; 55 (LO), Gabor Kovacs Photography/Shutterstock; 55 (LO LE), John Carnemolla/Shutterstock; 56-57, Tim Davis

ANTARCTICA
56, Adam Cropp/Getty Images; 58 (LO), Art Wolfe/Getty Images; 58 (LO LE), © 2005 Norbert Wu; 58 (UP), Kim Westerskov/STONE/Getty Images; 58 (UP RT), Ralph Lee Hopkins/National Geographic Image Collection; 59 (LO RT), Zaruba Ondrej/Shutterstock

Since 1888, the National Geographic Society has funded more than 12,000 research, exploration, and preservation projects around the world. The Society receives funds from National Geographic Partners, LLC, funded in part by your purchase. A portion of the proceeds from this book supports this vital work. To learn more, visit natgeo.com/info.

NATIONAL GEOGRAPHIC and Yellow Border Design are trademarks of the National Geographic Society, used under license.

For more information, visit nationalgeographic.com, call 1-800-647-5463, or write to the following address:

National Geographic Partners
1145 17th Street N.W.
Washington, D.C. 20036-4688 U.S.A.

Visit us online at nationalgeographic.com/books

For librarians and teachers: ngchildrensbooks.org

More for kids from National Geographic: natgeokids.com

National Geographic Kids magazine inspires children to explore their world with fun yet educational articles on animals, science, nature, and more. Using fresh storytelling and amazing photography, *Nat Geo Kids* shows kids ages 6 to 14 the fascinating truth about the world—and why they should care. **kids.nationalgeographic.com/subscribe**

For information about special discounts for bulk purchases, please contact National Geographic Books Special Sales: specialsales@natgeo.com

For rights or permissions inquiries, please contact National Geographic Books Subsidiary Rights: bookrights@natgeo.com

Designed by Kathryn Robbins

The publisher would like to thank everyone who worked to make this book come together: Martha Sharma, writer/researcher; Suzanne Fonda, project manager; Angela Modany, associate editor; Shannon Hibberd, senior photo editor; Mike McNey, map production; Scott A. Zillmer, map research and edit; Sean Philpotts, production director; Anne LeongSon and Gus Tello, design production assistants; Sally Abbey, managing editor, and Joan Gossett, production editor.

National Geographic supports K–12 educators with ELA Common Core Resources. Visit natgeoed.org/commoncore for more information.

Trade paperback ISBN: 978-1-4263-3552-5
Hardcover ISBN: 978-1-4263-3482-5
Reinforced library binding ISBN: 978-1-4263- 3483-2

Printed in Malaysia
19/IVM/1